High Performance Hiring

Selecting the Best

Revised Edition

Robert W. Wendover

A Crisp Fifty-Minute™ *Series Book*

This Fifty-Minute™ book is designed to be "read with a pencil." It is an excellent workbook for self-study as well as classroom learning. All material is copyright-protected and cannot be duplicated without permission from the publisher. *Therefore, be sure to order a copy for every training participant through our Web site, www.axzopress.com.*

High Performance Hiring

Selecting the Best

Revised Edition

Robert W. Wendover

CREDITS:
VP, Product Development: **Adam Wilcox**
Editor: **Brenda Pittsley**
Production Editor: **Genevieve McDermott**
Production Artists: **Nicole Phillips and Betty Hopkins**
Cartoonist: **Ralph Mapson**

ISBN 10: 1-56052-666-1
ISBN 13: 978-1-56052-666-7
Library of Congress Catalog Card Number 2002112498
Printed in the United States of America

4 5 6 7 09 08

Learning Objectives For:

HIGH PERFORMANCE HIRING

The objectives for *High Performance Hiring, Revised Edition* are listed below. They have been developed to guide the user to the core issues covered in this book.

THE OBJECTIVES OF THIS BOOK ARE TO HELP THE USER:

1) Identify the kind of employee who will succeed in the organization

2) Review laws governing fair hiring practices

3) Choose the right person for the job

ASSESSING PROGRESS

A Crisp Series **assessment** is available for this book. The 25-item, multiple-choice and true/false questionnaire allows the reader to evaluate his or her comprehension of the subject matter.

To download the assessment and answer key, go to www.axzopress.com and search on the book title.

Assessments should not be used in any employee selection process.

About the Author

Robert W. Wendover has been writing and speaking on the topic of hiring for the past 16 years. The author of five books, his work has appeared in publications as varied as *The Wall Street Journal's National Business Employment Weekly* and *Convenience Store News*. He appears regularly in electronic media including CNN, CNBC and an array of local stations around the U.S. His clients include Kinko's, Sears, State Farm Insurance, Kaiser Permanente, and a host of other household names. He has also served on the management faculty of the University of Phoenix for the past 10 years.

How to Use This Book

This *Fifty-Minute™ Series Book* is a unique, user-friendly product. As you read through the material, you will quickly experience the interactive nature of the book. There are numerous exercises, real-world case studies, and examples that invite your opinion, as well as checklists, tips, and concise summaries that reinforce your understanding of the concepts presented.

A Crisp *Fifty-Minute™ Series Book* can be used in a variety of ways. Individual self-study is one of the most common. However, many organizations use *Fifty-Minute* books for pre-study before a classroom training session. Other organizations use the books as a part of a systemwide learning program—supported by video and other media based on the content in the books. Still others work with Crisp to customize the material to meet their specific needs and reflect their culture. Regardless of how it is used, we hope you will join the more than 20 million satisfied learners worldwide who have completed a *Fifty-Minute Book*.

Preface

My, how things have changed! In the past 12 years, since this book was originally written, we have seen the advent of electronically scanned résumés, the proliferation of the Internet, the widespread use of job search engines, not to mention the introduction of the Americans with Disabilities Act and a host of other laws affecting the employer/employee relationship.

One thing remains the same, people hire people. While technology has overshadowed much of what is now done in business, it is still up to the hiring manager to make the best decision. But here, also, a lot has changed. American society has truly become the melting pot of the world. Employers report a marked decline in basic skills and a new generation has entered the workplace, in force, with another one on the way. New values and attitudes about work ethic have emerged. Language barriers have increased. The litigiousness of society is forcing compromises in the convictions of many managers. Those in the hiring seat face an entirely new set of challenges than those of a decade ago.

How has this book changed? In a variety of ways. The chapters on résumé screening and interviewing have been updated to include both technological factors and another 12 years of wisdom. In addition, the bibliography and resource information has been updated along with the addition of a new section on hiring those from other generations.

The one thing that has not changed is the down-to-earth approach I've taken to communicate what you, the manager or supervisor, need to know. After all, hiring the right people is the most important responsibility you have. So, no theory, no complicated processes, just the basic tools and strategies you need to select the perfect people for your team. Let's get on with it!

Robert W. Wendover

Contents

Part 5: Testing

Part 6: Conducting Reference Checks

Part 7: Decision Making and Offers

Summary

Finding and Retaining the Best

High performance hiring means selecting the best employees for your job openings. In a tight labor market, smart employers look to diverse population groups and use creative recruitment techniques to find quality employees.

Hiring is most effective when employers have a sufficient pool of high-caliber candidates from which to choose the best people for specific jobs. Achieving this optimal situation requires focus and organization on the part of the employer, plus a willingness to experiment with methods, research, and incentive programs. In doing this, it is important to remember that while you are evaluating prospective employees, they are also evaluating your company. A company that maintains a high profile and seems desirable to work for will attract more qualified candidates. Employee selection is not a one-sided event.

For tips on attracting the best people for your job openings, read *Recruiting for High Performance,* the companion title to this book, available from Crisp Publications.

The Impact of Turnover

Organizations spend a great deal of time recruiting and hiring new employees, but too few pay close attention to the cost of turnover. Only in recent years have industries examined the financial impact when an employee leaves, but the numbers are staggering. These estimates range from $4,200 for a supermarket checker to $35,000 for an account executive in financial services. Some may challenge these figures, so it is important to explain how they were calculated and their impact on bottom-line profit.

The cost of employee turnover can be divided into two categories, direct costs and opportunity costs. **Direct costs** include actual out-of-pocket recruiting, plus the time expended by staff and management. The Cost of Turnover memorandum on the next page demonstrates a typical breakdown of direct costs. **Opportunity costs** are the number of hours it takes for a new employee to fully acquire the skills and knowledge of the previous employee, plus the cost of mistakes this person makes along the way.

Another element to consider is the harm a terminated employee can do to an organization by alienating customers, wasting time, producing sloppy work, or causing damage through carelessness. While these costs are harder to calculate, they comprise the majority of the actual expense. Most studies estimate that opportunity costs exceed direct costs by a factor of four to one.

The cost of employee turnover has a direct impact on an organization's bottom line. To illustrate: If an organization employs 200 people and experiences a turnover of 20%, then it replaces 40 people per year. If the average replacement cost of an employee is $5,000, then the organization forfeits $200,000 in net profits. If the business has average sales transactions of $100, then 2,000 people must purchase products before the company realizes a profit. If the organization produces a 5% pre-tax net on its operations, then it would have to generate an additional $4,000,000 in sales to replace the lost profit due to employee turnover.

Turnover costs are insidious. Most managers do not pay attention to them and, in the end, rob themselves and their organization of thousands of dollars in bottom-line profit. In fact, more emphasis should be placed on employee retention than recruitment.

x

Memorandum

To: Alex Raski, Vice President

From: John Tutor, Customer Service Manager

Subject: Cost of Turnover

Here are the estimated costs for replacing a receptionist, as we did last week. It's obvious that this could get expensive if we have to do it again soon.

Exit interview with manager @ $20/hr	$20
Administrative paperwork @ $14/hr	14
Last day of work (exit interview, clean out desk, party, etc.) 8 hours@ $15/hr (incl. benefits)	120
New-hire selection costs (this has been our average)	863
Training (unproductive time for 20 hrs @ $14/hr)	280
	$1,297

Note: This does not include unemployment compensation if necessary.

The Hiring Skills Inventory

To examine the hiring and retention procedures in your organization, it is helpful to conduct a hiring skills inventory. The following questions address the major considerations of a successful hiring effort.

1 Have you defined the type of person who excels in your organization?

Examine the culture. What motivates your top performers? How well do people get along? Is this a serious atmosphere or is it more fun loving? How important are people skills in your business? Make a list of the characteristics you think are necessary for success in your organization. Share it with others and ask them to add their thoughts. The resulting factors comprise a checklist of what to look for in your new hires.

2 Are your hiring procedures consistent and well defined?

Employee selection that is conducted without clear procedures or performed in a haphazard way can result in high turnover, discrimination, and loss of your best applicants. Hiring need not be complicated, but it must have direction. Hiring also must be conducted with consistency. If candidates are treated in a variety of ways, they will be confused and frustrated. A clearly defined and timely succession of steps results in building a positive impression among your top candidates.

3 Is everyone involved well informed?

It is common to involve too many people in the hiring process. It does not take six people to hire a receptionist. A few key people should be responsible for screening applicants and making timely decisions. Those who screen individuals should know the job description, selection procedures, timetable, and regulations regarding the selection process. Do not assume that high-level managers are adept at hiring. Take the time to make sure this important process is explained to everyone.

4 Do you track hiring costs?

How much did it cost to replace the last receptionist who left the organization? With employee turnover running into thousands of dollars, no organization can afford to be sloppy with its hiring. Calculating turnover and recruiting costs bring home the seriousness of conducting employee selection with care.

5 Are you considering the versatility of candidates?

While most people are hired to perform one role, many end up doing a variety of tasks. Are you looking for individuals who readily adapt to new responsibilities and challenges?

6 Are you hiring "10s"?

Are you and your managers stretching yourselves to hire the best people available? Too often, managers tend to hire good followers as opposed to good potential leaders. While this strategy might make their lives easier in the short run, it can also hinder organizational growth. Impress upon managers that hiring staff with the drive to succeed will not only improve the company, it will make them look good too.

While this list is not all-inclusive, it should give you a working knowledge of the key components of high performance hiring. Notice that the points are not all mechanical. They involve focus, philosophy, and a general understanding of human nature. Selection processes that are too mechanical neglect the understanding needed to select not just a qualified person, but the right person for the job.

What Are You

Looking For?

2

The Role of Job Audits and Descriptions

Job descriptions serve two vital purposes. First, they define specific responsibilities, draw parameters, and provide a feel for the role a position plays within the greater organization. Second, job descriptions serve as benchmarks for measuring performance. As such, they can form the backbone of an organization's structure.

Job descriptions are smart for many reasons. For example, whenever a labor claim is investigated, a job description is usually requested as part of its investigation. Organizations that provide them can use them to protect their company from unfair claims. Written job descriptions are not required by law, but organizations that do not use them may seem unmindful of their employees' rights and responsibilities.

Traditionally, a job description outlined the necessary skills and qualifications to do a job, and then listed specific tasks and duties. Contemporary job descriptions consider these elements as well as more personal factors such as job pace or an ability to work well with other people. This change is due to an acknowledgment that these factors are as necessary to job success as technical skills or education. A job description for a restaurant host can explain that the position requires an enthusiastic personality and someone who is able to be efficient and pleasant while interacting with a wide variety of customers. A job description for a service representative can specify that applicants must be persevering, since they will have to track down complicated problems.

Providing Purpose

It is uncomfortable to not know what you're supposed to do at work. New employees ask themselves, "What is the purpose of my job?" "How does it fit into the system?" "What kind of power and influence does this position have?" "Am I doing the right things?" "How will I know when I'm doing a good job?" Job candidates ask variations of these same questions. A comprehensive job description provides answers and helps everyone feel more confident.

Developing clear expectations means being able to define, on paper, what an individual should be able to accomplish in a given position. Job descriptions should not be carved in stone, however. They should evolve with the changing needs of the organization. To this end, they should be reviewed and revised before positions are filled. Job descriptions are rarely followed to the letter, but they provide a benchmark from which to start.

Job descriptions also hold managers and employees accountable. In the hustle and bustle of business, it is easy to get absorbed in certain tasks to the neglect of other responsibilities. Job descriptions should not be used as weapons for keeping employees in line. However, they can be useful reminders of specific roles and responsibilities.

If your company already has job descriptions, now may be a good time to review them for accuracy. A job audit is a good way to do this. A job audit compares the tasks outlined with the actual duties being performed. Ask people in the job what they would change about the description.

Conducting a Job Audit

A job audit looks at an actual job and its relation to the entire organization. It seeks to answer questions such as: Does the job serve a valuable role in the company? Do the duties overlap those of other positions? Is this okay? Can parts of this job be eliminated or automated?

Consult with managers for their input. Ask them for insight on how the job could be better defined or improved. Do not attempt to conduct the audit without input from the jobholder. No one is closer to the job.

The following form is used to gather information about a specific job. The information will be used later to write a job description for the position. For the best results, have the jobholder answer the questions verbally in an interview format. The answers will be more realistic if another person is asking the questions. If more than one person holds a position, interview all of them and take an average of the responses.

JOB AUDIT FORM

Job title: _____   Dept.: _____

Audit conducted by: _____   Date: _____

Duties:

Major:

Minor:

Relationships (including number of employees supervised):

Training required:

Education/licenses/certifications:

Experience required (identify specific skills):

Physical requirements:

On-the-job hazards/working conditions:

Source of audit information:

Questions to Ask During a Job Audit

Here are some questions that a person who conducts a job audit interview can ask. The questions are designed to supply the information requested in the Job Audit Form.

➤ What duties do you perform? (Be specific in description.)

➤ What tools, services, or accommodations do you need to complete these duties?

➤ Who supervises this position?

➤ With whom do you interact, both in and out of the company?

➤ Are you able to complete all duties in the time allotted?

➤ What formal training do you need to perform this job, if any?

➤ What skills do you need to complete this job? (Include technical, interpersonal, organizational, and problem-solving skills.)

➤ How is your job performance evaluated?

The interviewer should be as specific as possible when completing the audit form. The following response is too vague:

Takes care of all inventory paperwork.

A better way to describe this duty is:

Responsible for the completion of all paperwork on incoming inventory. This includes, but is not limited to, checking manifests against actual counts, recording and assigning storage for all incoming freight, maintaining accurate control over all internal distribution of inventory. This responsibility entails 60% of average weekly time.

The second description gives a more complete and realistic picture of what the job entails.

In addition to interviewing the jobholders, examine the job's overall role in the organization. Look at factors such as role influence, customer contact, career path to other positions, and relationship to other functions within the same department. The more information gathered, the more complete the job audit will be. On the next page is an example of a completed job audit form.

JOB AUDIT FORM

Job title: Delivery Van Driver

Audit conducted by: Bob Elliott

Dept.: Transportation

Date: Sept. 3, (year)

Duties:

Major: Deliver packages to local customers. Sort packages for delivery. Inspect truck operations daily. Maintain good customer relations. Operate safely at all times. Complete all delivery paperwork.

Minor: Maintain truck. Clean truck on daily basis (interior once a day, exterior twice a week). Maintain updates to safety regulations in truck.

Relationships (including number of employees supervised):
Reports to transportation manager. Supervises no one. Occasionally trains new drivers.

Training required:
Training to drive step vans or similar vehicle. Ability to understand manifests and safety rules and traffic laws.

Education/licenses/certifications:
Valid chauffeur's license for this state.

Experience required (identify specific skills):
Three years experience driving step vans or similar vehicle. Very familiar with local streets. Ability to deal with customers in a positive manner.

Physical requirements:
Must be able to drive truck with manual brakes and steering. Lift up to 70 lbs.

On-the-job hazards/working conditions:
Normal hazards associated with driving a truck in local traffic. Potential lifting injuries.

Source of audit information: Interview with four current or former company drivers.

IS THIS JOB NECESSARY?

It is also a good idea to conduct a job audit for new positions. New employees represent long-term commitments, so it is valuable to look before you leap. The following questions examine the justifications for creating and filling a new position. Check (✔) the questions that will help you define whether a proposed position is necessary.

❑ What is the purpose of this new position?

❑ Who performs these tasks now?

❑ If the employees who presently perform this task are overtaxed, how long has this been a problem?

❑ Is the need for a new position driven by a short-term business cycle or is it the result of a long-term labor shortage?

❑ Is this a true need, or is it possible that existing responsibilities could be streamlined for better productivity?

❑ What will be the initial goals of this position and how long will it take to accomplish them?

❑ What is the best that can happen if we fill this position with a good person?

❑ Is there enough work for a full-time position? Can it be done by a part-time employee?

❑ How much will this new position cost?

❑ Is there a sufficient labor market to choose from?

❑ Will the need for this position exist 24 months from now?

❑ Is there broad agreement within the work group that the new position is necessary?

❑ How will other departments view adding this position? (They may feel their need is equally important.)

❑ Will this position result in tasks being removed from another position's responsibility list?

❑ What is the worst that can happen if we don't create this position?

Building a Job Description

Once an audit has been completed, a job description can be written with ease. Job descriptions should be reviewed at least once each year. This task should not be complicated unless there have been significant changes in the organization.

A job description is divided into the following parts:

➢ **Job summary**

➢ **Major duties**

➢ **Minor duties**

➢ **Relationships**

➢ **Qualifications**

➢ **Compensation**

The job summary is a brief, two- or three-sentence overview of the position. Major and minor duties consist of those functions delineated in the job audit. Major duties are those of primary concern that generally consume the majority of time. Minor duties are those that play a secondary role in how the job is performed. Relationships cover whom the position reports to and who, if anyone, reports to that position.

When filling openings for established positions, describe what needs to be done, not what is being done presently. This is because a present jobholder may be going above and beyond assigned duties or is underserving the position. Also include how the person filling the position will be evaluated.

Qualifications cover necessary skills, experience, and education. Be careful to list only those qualifications that are necessary. Necessary training is also included in this section.

The job description can include the compensation structure, such as commissions, hourly work, and eligibility for overtime. Actual rates should not be listed as they may change frequently. The Compensation Profile Form on the next page provides a list of factors to consider in the structuring of compensation. This form could be used to conduct a competitive analysis of your company's policies and offerings.

After drafting the job description, have anyone who is currently in the position review it for accuracy or omissions.

COMPENSATION PROFILE FORM

Type of Compensation	Present Policy	Competitor's Policy	How We Compare	Recommendations
Wages				
Salary increases				
Bonuses				
Profit sharing				
Flexible hours				
Paid vacation				
Paid holidays				
Paid sick leave				
Paid disability				
Other paid leave •Jury duty •Funeral •Military •Marriage •Pregnancy				
Health insurance				
Dental insurance				
Disability insurance				
Life insurance				
Pension plan				
Savings plan				
Credit union				
Education benefits				
Child benefits				
Elder care				
Other				

Using Job Descriptions in the Selection Process

A job description helps applicants understand the position and its role in the organization. See the sample job description below for an example.

Show the job description to each finalist. Make sure these individuals fully understand the job requirements. Give each an opportunity to fully examine it and ask questions. Rushing a person through this process defeats the purpose of finding the best possible candidate.

If you want to hire someone who does not quite fit the job description, don't be afraid to modify the job to fit the applicant. Now that you have a grasp of the positions you want to fill, it is time to examine the laws and statutes covering the hiring process.

JOB DESCRIPTION

Job title: Purchasing Manager

Job summary: Coordinates and approves all purchasing activities including the bidding process and office supplies budgeting.

Major duties: Coordinates overall purchasing effort for all corporate purchases of more than $100. Supervises bidding process on all corporate purchases of $500 or more. Serves as a purchasing resource for department managers and executives. Responsible for the accounting of all purchasing. Supervises purchasing staff.

Minor duties: Hires and trains all purchasing staff. Serves on corporate planning council. Maintains up-to-date catalogs and resources for purchasing needs. Prepares annual budget for purchasing department. Maintains relations with vendors as necessary.

Relationships: Reports to vice-president of operations. Supervises two purchasing specialists and one secretary.

Qualifications: Solid working knowledge of the purchasing process with a minimum of two years direct experience in purchasing and supervision of others. Substantial knowledge of budgeting including staffing costs. Excellent written, verbal, and negotiating skills.

Compensation: Commensurate with experience. Check current compensation charts for actual salary and benefits package.

Descriptions prepared by: _____ **Date:** _____

The Legal Side
of Hiring

14

Know the Law

In this litigious society, the laws regulating the selection of employees are of crucial concern. These laws were written to protect applicants and employees, and can result in considerable cost to employers if not followed. For the purposes of hiring, a working knowledge of federal, state, and local legislation is essential.

The philosophical reasons for enacting these laws included preventing discrimination and unjust treatment of employees or applicants. One must be careful, however, to note that the laws apply only to identified classes. White males under age 40, for example, are not a protected class. Individuals from an unprotected class may be protected in another class if they meet special criteria. For example, a Vietnam veteran might be protected under the Rehabilitation Act of 1973, but only when applying to an organization that falls under the Act's jurisdiction.

This is just one example of the complexities surrounding the employment process. New cases and variations are decided every day. The best rule of thumb is to look at every applicant with an unbiased eye. If an action looks discriminatory, it most likely is.

Having a company policy that renounces discrimination is not enough. If the company rejects discrimination on paper, but maintains an all-white management in a predominantly black community, for instance, it is in violation of Title VII of the Civil Rights Act of 1964.

With more than 400 federal laws pertaining to employee rights and selection, it would be counterproductive to discuss each one. Therefore, only the major laws and applications are covered here.

Federal Legislation

The **Civil Rights Act of 1964** is the cornerstone of antidiscrimination legislation in the United States. **Title VII** of this act covers labor and employment. It provides for the removal of artificial, arbitrary, and unnecessary barriers to employment when these barriers discriminate against individuals on the basis of race, sex, marital status, or religious beliefs. Title VII was amended in 1978 to include the Pregnancy Discrimination Act, which prohibits discrimination on the basis of childbirth, pregnancy, or related medical conditions.

The **Age Discrimination in Employment Act,** also amended in 1978, prohibits employers from discriminating in the hiring of individuals 40 years of age and older.

The **Rehabilitation Act of 1973** was enacted to prohibit discrimination against otherwise qualified handicapped individuals. This act only applies to employers holding federal contracts in excess of $2,500 or who receive financial assistance from the federal government.

The **Immigration Reform and Control Act** prohibits employers from hiring illegal aliens. It requires all new employees to produce specified documents proving they are legally eligible to work in the United States.

The **Fair Labor Standards Act,** as amended by the **Equal Pay Act,** sets minimum wages as well as overtime and equal pay standards.

The **Polygraph Protection Act** enacted in 1988 prohibited use of polygraphs and voiceprint devices.

The **Americans with Disabilities Act of 1990** prohibits discrimination against qualified individuals with disabilities in employment, public services, transportation, public accommodation, and telecommunications.*

The **Civil Rights Act of 1991** reestablishes the burden of proof on employers in cases of discrimination complaints and permits compensatory and punitive damages.

---

*For more information, read *The Americans with Disabilities Act* by Mary B. Dickson, a Crisp Series book.

Who Is Protected?

Title VII and the Americans with Disabilities Act apply to all private employers, state and local governments, educational institutions, and labor organizations that have 15 or more employees. Those individuals must have been employed every working day in each of 20 or more calendar weeks in the current or preceding calendar year. These same parameters apply to the Age Discrimination in Employment Act and the Pregnancy Discrimination Act of 1978.

The exception to these guidelines is the **Immigration Reform and Control Act (IRCA)**. Under this legislation, all new employees are required to show proof of their eligibility to work in the United States within the first three days of employment. Unlike Title VII and other antidiscrimination laws, IRCA includes all employers.

In addition to the federal government, many states have passed laws governing employment that parallel federal legislation. Since state laws are often broader, more comprehensive, and more stringent than federal statutes, it is paramount that everyone performing a hiring function be familiar with them. The most stringent law, whether federal, state, or local, is the one that applies.

The Equal Employment Opportunity Commission (EEOC) is charged with enforcing Title VII, the Pregnancy Discrimination Act, the Age Discrimination in Employment Act, the Equal Pay Act, the Americans with Disabilities Act, and the Civil Rights Act of 1991. It accomplishes this task through district offices throughout the United States.

The Rehabilitation Act of 1973 is enforced by the Office of Federal Contract Compliance Programs and each federal agency. The Immigration Reform and Control Act is enforced by the Immigration and Naturalization Service, although the law is written so that employers are responsible for enforcement within their own organizations.*

To assist employers in understanding the federal legislation covering employee selection, the EEOC issued the **Uniform Guidelines for Employee Selection Procedures in 1978.** The questions asked by an employer cannot be deemed unlawful. What the employer does with the answers can be called into question.

An interviewer might say, for example, "That's quite an accent you've got. Where does it come from?" While the actual intent may be innocent, the interviewer's question could be interpreted as a judgment that this person should not be hired due to his or her heritage. Every interview question must have a business necessity. If the position being filled is one involving significant customer contact, for example, a question regarding the accent might be acceptable if it impairs the person's ability to communicate in English. The more appropriate tactic in this instance would be to engage that person in a discussion about customer service to determine how well the applicant communicates.

There are a few instances where an employer can set a standard restricting the employment of a certain group. These requirements are called **Bona Fide Occupational Qualifications (BFOQ)**, and are based on business necessity.

A typical example would be restricting men from serving in certain areas of a health club that are private to female patrons. Since BFOQs are severely limited, the best policy is to assume there are no exceptions. Apply each hiring requirement as if all applicants are eligible.

Affirmative Action

Affirmative action is the action taken by an employer to ensure equal opportunity for all protected groups. Affirmative action programs detail the ways in which this commitment is carried out. While not all employers are required to have a formal program, policies are developed for one of three reasons:

1. As a voluntary commitment to equal opportunity

2. As mandated by federal law (**Executive Order 11246** requires all federal contractors and subcontractors and recipients of federal funds of $50,000 or more to develop and implement a written affirmative action program monitored by the Department of Labor.)

3. As required, because of discriminatory practices and/or impacts on protected classes

An affirmative action program includes the following objectives:

➤ Establishing a company policy and commitment to equal opportunity

➤ Identifying positions in the company where those in protected classes are underutilized

➤ Setting specific, measurable, and attainable goals for hiring and promotion within each area of the company, with target dates for completion

➤ Reviewing all hiring criteria to be sure they are legitimate requirements of the job

➤ Making concerted efforts to locate qualified persons in protected classes who meet job requirements or who can be trained to do so

➤ Informing all managers and supervisors that they are accountable for helping to achieve the objectives of the affirmative action program

➤ Assigning one top company official the responsibility and authority for the program and its progress

Key components of affirmative action:

1. An employer is not required to establish an affirmative action program unless it has shown past discrimination. The exception is contractors having $50,000 in federal contracts and more than 50 employees.

2. There must be a clear assignment of who will direct the program. A senior executive is usually required to fill this role.

3. The plan must have clearly stated procedures.

4. The plan must contain a clearly stated equal opportunity policy.

5. The plan must contain specific goals and timetables for hiring from protected groups who are underrepresented.

Once an affirmative action program is in place, it is the organization's responsibility to actively recruit members of protected classes for present and future openings. This recruitment can be accomplished in a variety of ways, including:

➤ Establishing relations with nearby colleges and job services to keep them informed of your staffing needs

➤ Attending job fairs in the local area

➤ Placing advertisements in periodicals that attract large numbers of women and minorities

➤ Using female and minority recruiters

➤ Using photographs of women and minorities in advertisements

➤ Holding informational tours of the company for specified groups

Merely having the appropriate number of protected-class employees in your firm does not accomplish affirmative action. These individuals must be qualified for the positions they hold. If they are not, training arrangements should be made to qualify them if other suitable candidates cannot be found. Examining agencies scrutinize an organization's practices, not just the end results.

Establishing and completing an affirmative action program is a complex task requiring commitment from the entire organization. For additional information, qualified experts should be consulted.

Avoiding Adverse Impact

Under Title VII of the Civil Rights Act of 1964, an employer's hiring practices become illegal when the company operates to the disadvantage of certain protected classes of individuals. While the employment practices may be neutral in appearance and intent, the company's hiring practices must reflect the characteristics of the surrounding community.

A number of variables enter into this equation, such as the ratios of employees within the organization and the population of certain protected classes within the surrounding community. It is best to keep accurate records of hiring patterns, regardless of your organization's size.

Avoiding Discrimination

The key element in deciding whether a particular requirement can be considered a hiring condition is whether the requirement is related to or required by the job. While some requirements can be clearly identified as discriminatory, others have an impact on certain protected classes but are not obviously discriminatory. The more common job requirements are listed below along with whether or when they might be allowed. Check your hiring policies to see if your company is in compliance with these standards:

Accents: Candidates may be excluded from a position if that position requires substantial communication with customers and/or employees and the person's accent is found to be so strong that it would impair that person's performance.

Age requirements: Under the Age Discrimination in Employment Act, employers may not discriminate on the basis of age except in situations where there is a bona fide occupational qualification.

Employment of aliens: Aliens must have permission to work in the United States. Employers are responsible for checking an employee's eligibility to work within three days of hire.

Alienage: An employer cannot require citizenship as a standard for hire under Title VII of the Civil Rights Act of 1964. Exceptions to this rule usually revolve around national security.

Appearance and dress: Applicants cannot be rejected on the basis of appearance and dress, if the appearance and dress is typical of their culture. Employers can set dress standards if there is a business necessity such as safety requirements.

Arrest and criminal records: Arrest records cannot be used as a basis for rejecting an applicant. Employers are prohibited from rejecting an applicant on the basis of a conviction, unless that conviction is substantially related to job responsibilities. An applicant who has been convicted of shoplifting, for instance, can be refused a job as a security guard.

Blacklisting: Most states prohibit blacklisting of applicants for any reason.

Credit requirement: Employers may not require an acceptable credit rating as a condition for employment unless they can demonstrate a business necessity, such as in the hiring of a cashier or financial manager.

Dependent's status: If no such requirement exists for male applicants, an employer cannot reject a female candidate because she has children of pre-school age. Nor can a woman be refused employment because she is a single parent, since this factor is not related to business necessity.

Disabilities: Employers are subject to the Rehabilitation Act of 1973 if they receive grants from the federal government or have federal contracts in excess of $2,500 annually. Under this Act, an employer is required to provide reasonable accommodation to applicants with disabilities. This may include wheelchair access, removal of architectural barriers, adjustments of furniture and equipment, and special aids for telephones.

Employers with 15 or more employees are subject to the Americans with Disabilities Act of 1990 (ADA). ADA requirements mirror those of the Rehabilitation Act.

The courts have held that disabilities are not limited to common physical impairments. They also may include obesity, suicidal tendencies, borderline personality, posttraumatic stress syndrome, diabetes, and allergies to tobacco smoke. Alcoholics and drug addicts are also considered handicapped unless their condition currently prevents them from performing a job. The majority of states have also decided that Acquired Immune Deficiency Syndrome (AIDS) is a physical handicap entitled to protection.

Education: Employers may require a certain level or type of education as a requirement only if it can be demonstrated to be a business necessity. A high school diploma can be required, for example, if the employer can demonstrate that the skills learned in high school are substantially necessary to perform the job.

Fingerprinting: Fingerprinting of applicants is generally accepted in all states except New York, where there are some limitations.

Gender: Males or females may not be precluded from a position unless the employer has a bona fide occupational qualification. Men, for example, may be restricted from women's locker room jobs.

Hair requirement: Employers may not have gender-specific hair requirements.

Health requirements: If an applicant fails a physical examination, the employer may refuse employment, provided that the requirements in the exam demonstrate that the applicant would not be able to perform the job.

Height/weight requirement: An employer can require a certain height or weight standard if it can be demonstrated to be a business necessity. Requiring flight attendants to meet a height requirement, for example, has been found to be a business necessity because of safety considerations.

Language requirement: If an employer can demonstrate that speaking English or another language is a business necessity for a particular job, then proficiency in that language may be required.

Marital status: An employer may not have a policy prohibiting the employment of married women, unless the same policy applies to married men.

Military record: Applicants may not be rejected on the basis of having a less-than-honorable military discharge, unless the employer can demonstrate the decision was related to job performance.

National origin: An applicant may not be rejected because of national origin, unless the employer can demonstrate a bona fide occupational qualification.

Nepotism: Prohibiting nepotism may be in violation of Title VII if it results in discriminatory impact on one or more protected classes. For example, if the major employer in a small town with a large minority population prohibits hiring employees' relatives, this may result in disparate impact.

No-spouse requirement: An employer may prohibit the hiring of a spouse providing the rule is neutral. In other words, if the wife of a male employee cannot be hired, the husband of a female employee cannot be hired.

Polygraph/lie detector: Employers are prohibited from using polygraphs, voice-print devices, and other related technology in the selection of employees. Major exceptions to this law are certain defense, security, and pharmaceutical jobs.

Pregnancy: An employer may not discriminate against women affected by pregnancy, childbirth, or related medical conditions.

Recruitment: There are no specific prohibitions regarding the recruitment of employees, but an employer who grants preferential treatment to friends, relatives, or employee referrals, for example, may be in violation of Title VII if protected classes are underrepresented.

Religious conviction: Reasonable accommodation must be made for an applicant's religious convictions, and the employer may not reject the applicant on that basis, unless it would cause undue hardship. An applicant, for example, who asks that an interview be moved because of the observance of a religious holiday should not suffer in the selection process because of this request.

Strength requirement: Provided the requirement is a business necessity, an employer can ask applicants to pass a strength test. An auto mechanic position might have this requirement if the employer can demonstrate its legitimacy.

Testing (aptitude/psychological): Employers may not require applicants to submit to aptitude or psychological testing unless they can demonstrate relatedness to job performance. Tests must be validated and be approved by the EEOC. They must not have an unequal impact on protected classes.

Testing (drugs and alcohol): There are no laws prohibiting drug testing at present. Issues around invasion of privacy, discriminatory impact, and accuracy are still being debated. It is best to have a well-defined policy in place before testing is initiated.

Work experience: Applicants may be required to have particular work experiences and skills, provided the employer can demonstrate business necessity. The amount of experience must be reasonable.

Negligent Hiring

The concept of negligent hiring is a new concern for employers. Under this theory, employers who know or should have known that an employee is unfit for a position may be liable for the employee's criminal or devious behavior. Negligent hiring is now recognized as cause of action in more than 30 states.

Generally, an employer has a duty to exercise reasonable care when hiring employees who, if incompetent or unreliable, might cause a risk of injury to the public or fellow employees by reason of their employment. Examples of this theory have been illustrated by court cases in which an employee used a passkey to enter an apartment and attack a tenant.

For more information, read *Rightful Termination* by Ron Visconti and Richard Stiller, a Crisp Series book.

State and Local Legislation

State laws are generally more comprehensive and restrictive than federal statutes. Employers must comply with all federal, state, and local laws affecting their locale.

If you are unfamiliar with them, become acquainted with the state laws affecting hiring. While there is no federal legislation regarding AIDS, for example, a number of large cities now have antidiscrimination laws covering those afflicted.

Most state antidiscrimination legislation takes affect with three or more employees. Title VII, however, does not affect an employer with fewer than 15 employees.

Examine all parts of the hiring process to ensure you are obeying the laws. This effort includes applications, interviews, record keeping, and job postings. States and municipalities vary significantly in their legislation and enforcement. Be sure you are aware of your organization's obligations.

All complaints must be filed with the EEOC along with the state agency. EEOC, however, defers its investigation for 60 days. If the state chooses to investigate, the EEOC will await the outcome before deciding to act.

P A R T 3

Reviewing Résumés and Applications

The Role of Résumés and Applications

How effectively do you review résumés and applications? Are you getting the information you need to reach a clear hiring decision?

While these documents are a significant factor in screening candidates, they are sometimes given too much emphasis in the hiring process. Résumés and applications must be viewed with skepticism. Studies show that as many as 30% of all applicants exaggerate or misrepresent themselves on these documents. Even so, you can make the most of these submissions by following some simple guidelines.

Recognize the different roles résumés and applications play. While some companies use them interchangeably, résumés traditionally have been required for professional positions. Applications have been relegated to the areas of skilled and unskilled labor.

Résumés give applicants the opportunity to express themselves in what they consider the best light possible. You might compare résumés to newspaper advertisements. Both showcase a product, and how they are designed greatly influences the viewer's opinion. Studies show that the average résumé screener spends less than 45 seconds reviewing a résumé before deciding the fate of its owner.

Applications provide information in a more rigid form. Any gaps in information are immediately noticed. The information is easy to interpret since it is presented in the same order on each submission.

Before deciding whether to ask for résumés or applications, consider criteria by which applicants will be screened. If you are looking for creative, self-reliant individuals, résumés will give you a better picture of their capacities. If you are hiring for assembly work, applicants' abilities to complete an application according to directions may be a deciding factor on whether to hire them.

Reviewing a Résumé

Determine your hiring criteria before you review a résumé. Simply looking for interesting facts and data will confuse the focus of who you should hire. List the optimal criteria, keeping in mind that you will not find the perfect candidate.

After determining criteria, you might want to create a checklist against which you can compare each applicant's qualifications. Make this a simple, easy-to-read document that provides reliable information for comparison. You might even build in a scoring system.

When reviewing résumés, break the examination into five categories:

➤ **Overall appearance**   ➤ **Experience**

➤ **Organization**   ➤ **Other relevant activities**

➤ **Education/training**

Overall Appearance

The overall appearance of the résumé gives you an idea of how much care was taken in its preparation, and the level of interest the applicant has in the job.

➤ Are there errors in spelling or grammar?

➤ Is the printing readable?

➤ Is it printed on good quality paper (with an envelope to match)?

➤ Does it have a "textbook" appearance, as if the format was copied directly from a book?

Organization

Does the résumé provide the information you need? Is it apparent that the applicant included the data most critical to helping you decide? (In other words, is this person anticipating your needs?) Does the résumé provide a clear path to the information, or is there no rhyme or reason to it? Can you understand the individual entries? A well-organized résumé probably means the applicant is well organized on the job. You can also assume that this person can communicate adequately in other situations.

Education / Training

When reviewing education qualifications, keep in mind that only relevant education may be considered. You cannot, for example, refuse employment to management applicants simply because they do not have college degrees. If you did, you would have to demonstrate how those applicants would not be able to handle the job solely for that reason. Instead, you need to establish a level of experience comparable to a degree and evaluate on that basis.

In addition to reviewing résumés for necessary qualifications, examine the motivations of someone with too much education who is applying for the position. Is this applicant truly interested in the position or just using it as a way station before moving on? If you do pass this person on to the next step in the hiring, that question needs to be answered in the interview.

Be flexible with college majors. While applicants may not have completed the exact course work akin to job requirements, this does not mean they can't handle the job. For instance, an English major might perform very well in a management role. Technical applications may require certain courses of study, but flexibility in accepting a variety of majors and educational backgrounds broadens your field of applicants.

Remember to check all educational credentials with the granting institution. Unfortunately, some applicants fabricate their education as needed.

Experience

In many cases, an applicant's experience may be critical to whether that person can do the job. Be careful, however, of excluding candidates because they do not match the exact experience requirements. Hiring a person who fully meets the job's qualifications may be counterproductive, since that person may be bored with no new challenges.

When you review the experience section of a résumé, consider the following:

➤ Does the applicant list duties versus responsibilities? (What was actually done?)

➤ Is there a list of accomplishments? It's easy to do some jobs without really contributing. How do you know this person made a difference?

➤ How long did the applicant hold each position? It is commendable if a person moved progressively upward in a short time. It can also spell impatience and disloyalty. The applicant might be unable to hold a job and is "dressing up" later job titles. Be careful to verify facts.

➤ If the person has held the same job for a number of years it can suggest stability or loyalty. On the other hand, it may suggest being too set in one's ways.

➤ Are the job titles authentic? The titles people use and the ones their employers use might be different. When challenged, the applicant might say, "Well, they called me a clerk, but I really did a manager's job." That may be true, but check it out.

➤ Does the applicant demonstrate how acquired skills fit into the position sought? Can you see the transferability of skills? Are parameters provided so you can see the extent of responsibility? These parameters might include number of staff supervised, control over budget, or size of sales goals met.

As you review this material, compare résumé information with your ideal candidate. No one will meet all of the qualifications, but it will be a good place to begin.

Other Relevant Activities

You may find a wide variety of information in this category. These might include college activities, community involvement, awards, church-related functions, hobbies, and participation in sports. All of these provide insight into applicant's personality and character. Many of the skills learned in school or community activities can be transferred to the place of work. Leadership positions in high school or college assist a person in developing the insight and understanding of work roles. Participation in sports promotes confidence. Other outside activities develop maturity and character.

SAMPLE RÉSUMÉ

Below is a sample résumé annotated to show how this information might be interpreted by a potential employer.

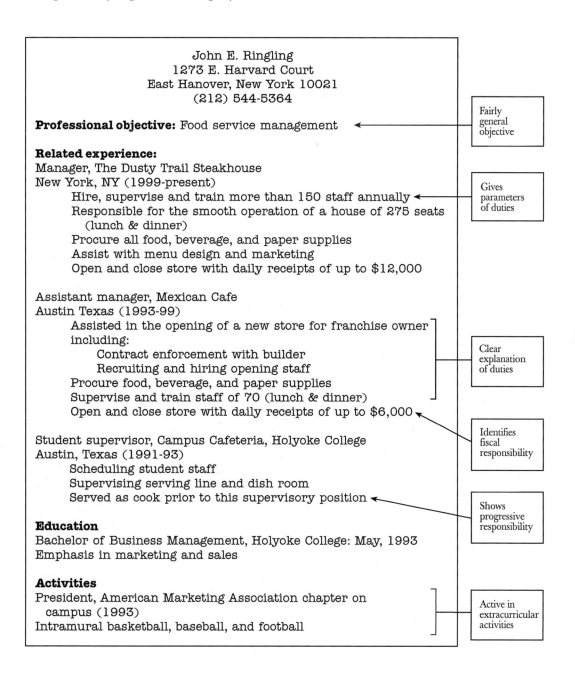

John E. Ringling
1273 E. Harvard Court
East Hanover, New York 10021
(212) 544-5364

Professional objective: Food service management

Fairly general objective

Related experience:
Manager, The Dusty Trail Steakhouse
New York, NY (1999-present)
    Hire, supervise and train more than 150 staff annually
    Responsible for the smooth operation of a house of 275 seats
      (lunch & dinner)
    Procure all food, beverage, and paper supplies
    Assist with menu design and marketing
    Open and close store with daily receipts of up to $12,000

Gives parameters of duties

Assistant manager, Mexican Cafe
Austin Texas (1993-99)
    Assisted in the opening of a new store for franchise owner
    including:
        Contract enforcement with builder
        Recruiting and hiring opening staff
    Procure food, beverage, and paper supplies
    Supervise and train staff of 70 (lunch & dinner)
    Open and close store with daily receipts of up to $6,000

Clear explanation of duties

Identifies fiscal responsibility

Student supervisor, Campus Cafeteria, Holyoke College
Austin, Texas (1991-93)
    Scheduling student staff
    Supervising serving line and dish room
    Served as cook prior to this supervisory position

Shows progressive responsibility

Education
Bachelor of Business Management, Holyoke College: May, 1993
Emphasis in marketing and sales

Activities
President, American Marketing Association chapter on
  campus (1993)
Intramural basketball, baseball, and football

Active in extracurricular activities

Electronic Options for Résumé Screening

Some businesses receive stacks of résumés in the mail each day from jobseekers hoping to win a position with the organization. Unfortunately, these résumés can get buried under paperwork, routed to the wrong department, or generally lost in the system. In the past decade or so, employers who deal with a high number of résumés have turned to computer software to better manage these applications. Here's how the system works:

When résumés arrive in the mail, they are electronically scanned using optical character recognition software. This produces an electronic document, which is compared to the original by a clerk who makes any necessary corrections to information that was incorrectly translated by the scanner. The clerk then assigns a series of codes to the scanned document identifying the position being sought, applicant's qualifications, and other information relevant to the organization's needs. This scanned résumé is then electronically stored in a database for retrieval at a later time.

When managers seek candidates for a position, they complete a form identifying the necessary qualifications. This information is used to search for appropriate résumés. The documents are then forwarded electronically to the managers for review. When managers select the candidates they would like to interview, the résumés can be printed out.

This system has a number of advantages:

➤ It eliminates the paperwork nightmare of handling actual résumés

➤ Fewer résumés from attractive candidates fall through the cracks simply because the organization is not hiring at the time they are received

➤ Staff is freed to work on other projects

➤ The software can provide data for compliance filings such as affirmative action

➤ Organizations can give candidates better quality service by sending a letter of response immediately after a résumé is received

➤ It allows human resources staff to respond quickly to managers' requests for résumés

The cost of implementing such a system runs anywhere from $30,000 to $75,000 depending on a variety of factors including hardware expense, scanning speed, software features, number of users, and storage capacity. While not for every organization, résumé scanning can save time and money for employers accepting large numbers of résumés.

Evaluating Cover Letters

The purpose of cover letters is to provide tailored presentations of an applicants' background relative to your organization. As such, they provide insight into an applicant's attitudes and abilities to do the job.

Things to look for when reviewing cover letters:

➤ Is it an original letter? Does it refer to your organization or previous contact with you? Is there evidence that the applicant researched your company prior to making contact?

➤ Is the spelling and grammar correct? These factors demonstrate basic skills and show care.

➤ Is it written in proper business format? Is it well typed on clean, crisp paper? These factors also show care and respect for the process.

➤ Is the letter addressed to you or another person within the organization? Does it begin anonymously with "Dear Sir or Madam"? This again reflects on the applicant's level of interest.

➤ Does the letter achieve its objective? Does the writer get the point across? Does it blend focus with persuasiveness?

Every evaluator has a different set of preferences when reviewing correspondence. The best strategy is to use your instincts while keeping an open mind.

SAMPLE COVER LETTER

Here is an evaluation of a sample cover letter:

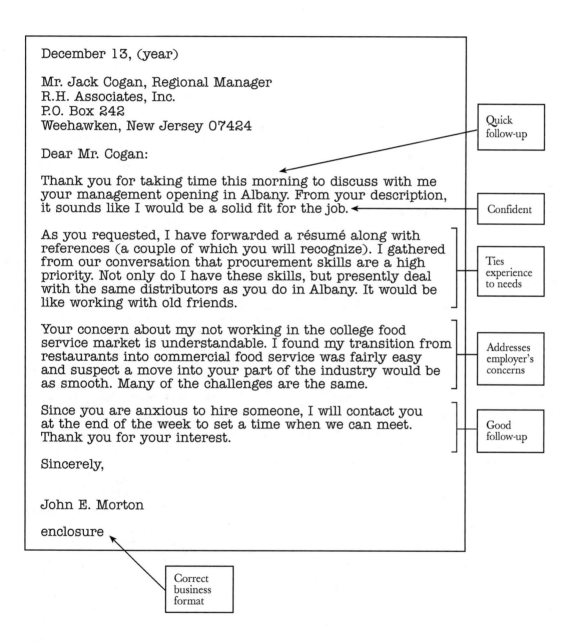

December 13, (year)

Mr. Jack Cogan, Regional Manager
R.H. Associates, Inc.
P.O. Box 242
Weehawken, New Jersey 07424

Dear Mr. Cogan:

Thank you for taking time this morning to discuss with me your management opening in Albany. From your description, it sounds like I would be a solid fit for the job.

As you requested, I have forwarded a résumé along with references (a couple of which you will recognize). I gathered from our conversation that procurement skills are a high priority. Not only do I have these skills, but presently deal with the same distributors as you do in Albany. It would be like working with old friends.

Your concern about my not working in the college food service market is understandable. I found my transition from restaurants into commercial food service was fairly easy and suspect a move into your part of the industry would be as smooth. Many of the challenges are the same.

Since you are anxious to hire someone, I will contact you at the end of the week to set a time when we can meet. Thank you for your interest.

Sincerely,

John E. Morton

enclosure

Quick follow-up

Confident

Ties experience to needs

Addresses employer's concerns

Good follow-up

Correct business format

Reviewing an Application

Comparing candidates is easier when they all complete the same application. This methods means applicants are treated consistently and information is accurately presented.

As you review an application, try to put all the information into perspective. If an applicant has two years of experience and the job description requires three, the person still may be eligible when factors such as education or special training are considered.

The key to reviewing applications is to have a clear picture of what the job entails. Could someone who does not meet the exact qualifications still be considered because of enthusiasm and desire? This clear picture also helps highlight inappropriate applicants who are trying to slip through the system. Look at the top qualifications necessary to do the job; they are your priority.

When reviewing applications, you can break the evaluation into five categories:

- ➤ **Clarity**

- ➤ **Cleanliness**

- ➤ **Legibility**

- ➤ **Experience**

- ➤ **Education**

Clarity

How clear are the explanations and answers to questions? Did the applicant rush through the form, or take the time to do it right? Were instructions followed? Were questions understood and answered with relevant information? (If you begin to see a number of applications where questions were misunderstood, you should review the application itself.)

Cleanliness

Was care taken to keep the application clean and neat? Was it folded up and stuck in a pocket? Does it have smudges and ink or food stains on it? Characteristics such as these indicate how organized and careful the applicant may be on the job.

Legibility

Is the handwriting readable? Does it fit in the lines? Are there a lot of crosscuts or erasures? (This can indicate that the applicant is altering information.) Can you understand what is being expressed? All of these factors comment on the applicant's care and diligence.

Experience

Does the experience offered match the experience required for the job? How is it explained? Can you get a good idea of a person's duties from their description? Does it sound reasonable? Remember that many skills are transferable. Be careful not to dismiss a qualified candidate because the match is not exact.

Education

As with experience, you need to check for credibility. Does the information seem consistent? Are the courses relevant to what you are looking for? Has this person completed certain levels of education? This indicates follow-through.

Remember, only job-related facts may be evaluated! For instance, the handwriting might be illegible or there might be a number of spelling errors. These factors can be considered only if the job requires legible writing and communication skills, such as completing forms or writing reports.

Electronic Applications

The process of accepting applications took some new turns with the advent of electronic mail. Jobs are being posted on the Internet and e-mail addresses are listed with contact information in promotions. Any candidate can now access an organization instantaneously.

While this can be a blessing, it also presents some significant challenges. Savvy applicants will research your organization on the Internet before contacting you to determine whether they should bother to apply. You may find that some applicants possess more knowledge about the overall organization than you do.

Because of the speed of e-mail, most applicants expect a faster response to their inquiries than they would with mail. The ability to "buy" time in the selection process has been diminished. This, coupled with a long-term low unemployment rate, may force the selection process to move faster than you want it to.

For certain positions, especially in information systems and engineering, advertising through the Internet may be an effective means of recruiting, but the number of applications can be overwhelming to the person(s) on your staff receiving all of this information.

GUIDELINES FOR ACCEPTING ELECTRONIC APPLICATIONS

1 Funnel all applications to a particular Web site or e-mail address.

Individual supervisors who post their own e-mail addresses may find themselves inundated with résumés or applications.

2 Develop a Web site, or at least a Web page specifically for accepting applications and résumés.

Promote your company's site in locations where applicants can click on a link, which connects them to a menu-driven process for applying. For examples of this process, explore Web sites owned by the nation's household name companies such as Pepsi-Cola, Boeing, and Wal-Mart.

3 Install an auto-responder on the site.

Auto-responders can automatically provide applicants with an overview of the selection process, an explanation of the hiring schedule, directions to interview locations along with information about the organization. Auto-responders allow you to be consistent in what you provide and confirms that the application or résumé has been received.

4 Coach receptionists and other front-line staff to give out only the company Web address, not individual e-mails addresses.

This protects individual managers from being inundated with applications and it allows the organization to comply with federal affirmative action requirements.

5 Be specific in your requirements when posting positions.

The easiest way to do this is to post the job descriptions for available positions. Applicants can print these out and respond to the individual requirements. You might even encourage them to do so. You can also indicate your level of flexibility on certain requirements, allowing them to make an informed decision as whether to apply. Remember, it is not the quantity of applicants that is important, but the quality.

Narrowing the List

Once you gather a number of applications or résumés, create a simple form with pertinent criteria listed across the top and the applicants' names down one side. This visual organization will help you make a clear comparison. You might develop a weighted scale, such as 1 to 5, and make your initial selections according to a cut-off level. See the Applicant Screen Form below for an example. Be careful not to be too strict. You don't want to eliminate good candidates before you speak with them. Consistency and impartiality are the keys to this process.

APPLICANT SCREENING FORM

Position title: _____   **Date:** _____

Screener: _____

Rate each applicant's résumé/application on the characteristics below according to the following scales:

1 = Does not meet expectations

2 = Meets expectations

3 = Exceeds expectations

4 = Outstanding

Applicant	Total
_____	____
_____	____
_____	____
_____	____
_____	____
_____	____

The Value of Telephone Screening

Apart from résumés and applications, a telephone call is usually your first contact with an applicant. While the amount of information obtainable through a phone call is limited, there is much to learn about a person's background, confidence level, communication skills, and a host of other things. Listen for the subtle things applicants reveal about themselves as they talk. You'll begin to paint the picture you need for your evaluation of this applicant.

But remember that just as you are evaluating applicants, they are evaluating you. How was the phone answered? How long did they wait on hold? Was the person they called prepared to answer their questions? Was the interviewer professional and courteous? Did the person seem rushed and harried? As with any part of the applicant selection process, the applicant and the recruiter are developing a relationship.

Preparing to Screen by Telephone

As you prepare to screen applicants, consider how they will apply for openings at your company. Will they submit résumés? Will they come in person to complete an application? Or will they call upon seeing the job advertisement?

Having applicants call may appear to be difficult and time-consuming. But proper organization enables you to use the call-in technique to shorten the screening process considerably. For example, applicants who call can be screened immediately. Those who pass the phone test are invited to send in a résumé. This is more efficient than having them send in a résumé first if you recognize that 50% or more of applicants are typically eliminated upon submission. Therefore, taking five to 10 minutes to screen each caller may eliminate a good deal of effort later.

PREPARATION CHECKLIST FOR TELEPHONE SCREENING

Here are a few suggestions if you choose to screen applicants over the phone after accepting applications:

❑ **Know the job.** If you supervise the position, this is a given. If, on the other hand, you screen for a number of positions, you should acquaint yourself with the job's current duties and responsibilities.

❑ **Develop clearly worded questions and outline what you expect for answers.** Try the questions on people inside the company to make sure they are understandable and elicit the type of answers you seek.

❑ **Obtain input from those who will work with the new person.** Even if you supervise the position being filled, you will not be the only person to work with the new hire. Soliciting suggestions and input from others will yield some good ideas and build their investment in hiring the right person for the job.

❑ **Prepare an evaluation form to be used for all applicants.** Notes on a legal pad do not provide the same clarity as a form that gives a summary of experience in the same place for each applicant.

❑ **Prepare what you will say about the job and the organization when screening applicants.** The best applicants for any position are talking with more than one employer. How you represent the job and your organization may determine the quality of the applicants you hire.

❑ **Prepare for common questions.** Brainstorm a list of questions that applicants are most likely to ask. Your preparation will put them at ease and demonstrate that you are truly concerned about hiring the right match for the job.

❑ **Rehearse the screening process.** Take the time to call a couple of co-workers and go through the process to iron out glitches. Appearing well prepared will make a positive impression on the best candidates.

❑ **Block out time to screen applicants so you will not be interrupted.** Nothing is more irritating to an applicant than to be put on hold while the interviewer handles other work. Showing applicants you respect their time will help lure the best to your business.

❑ **Give call-in applicants a good impression.** The reception applicants receive when they first respond to a job notice is critical to beginning the process on the right foot. A person answering the phone who seems to know nothing about the job can harm the way applicants perceive the company. Here are a few tips for ensuring that applicants are accorded the proper attention:

❑ **Prepare the receptionist.** With all the responsibilities a receptionist deals with during a normal day, it is easy to understand how fielding calls from applicants will seem like an unwanted distraction. Take the time to explain how critical first impressions are when attracting new employees. Give the receptionist clear instructions on what to say and how to refer applicants to the proper person.

❑ **Obtain the name, address and telephone number of every applicant.** Regardless of whether the person is to be hired, contact information should be recorded for every person who applies. In some cases, this may be a legal requirement, such as maintaining affirmative action logs. In other cases, there may be new openings in which previous applicants may have an interest.

❑ **Make sure each call is handled professionally.** Reinforce the receptionist's skill at answering the phone. With positive feedback, a receptionist is more likely to treat those calling you with more respect and friendliness.

❑ **Walk through the process.** Try giving your receptionist a couple of sample situations to see how they are handled. In some cases, you may have friends call in as applicants to learn how they are received.

Twelve Tips for Conducting Telephone Screening

As employers, we hope that hiring somebody will be the beginning of a long relationship. Both the organization and the applicant are making a big commitment. It is critical, therefore, to make the most of every screening situation. Here are some tips for maximizing the way you screen applicants on the telephone:

1 Develop rapport.

Just as you would in a formal interview, take a minute to put applicants at ease when you call. You might begin by asking how they found out about the job. If it was a referral, you might get into a short chat about that person.

2 Explain the position's duties up front.

Begin the interview by telling the applicant about the position and how it fits within the organization. Ask applicants to comment on ways their background fits the job as you ask some questions.

3 Take notes.

Do not rely on your memory to recall all the information the applicant gives you. Jotting down a few key words here and there will help you complete the evaluation form at the end of the interview. You might also jot down follow-up questions as they come up during the conversation.

4 Listen to what the applicant says and how it is said.

While you listen to the words, look for level of confidence, organization of thought, consistency of focus. Even though the person is not sitting in front of you, there are still many ways you can pick up on communication signals.

5 Treat everyone the same.

While you will identify with some applicants more than others, all applicants should receive the same level of attention and consistent message. Simply because you went to the same high school does not mean some applicants should get special treatment, especially if they are not right for the job.

6 Ask everyone the same questions.

It is easy to wander off the mark, especially if you get engrossed in a particular topic. It is difficult, however, to make clear comparisons if you have gathered only partial information on some applicants. Take the time to pursue items you think are important, but be sure to cover all the topics you need to.

7 Take your time.

Applicants can detect whether or not you are in a rush. While you may have a million things on your mind, taking the time to concentrate on the applicant will produce a better interview and demonstrate that you really do care about who you hire.

8 Question inconsistencies in what the applicant says.

Do not hesitate to ask about comments that seem inconsistent. Those who shy away from potentially uncomfortable situations lose the opportunity to truly filter only the best people into the rest of the process.

9 Use silence as a tool.

One of the most powerful strategies any interviewer has available is silence. Since most people are uncomfortable with a long silence, they tend to reveal more than they had planned. Sometimes the answer after the silence is more to the point.

10 Take time to answer the applicant's questions.

While there will be more time to answer questions if they make it in to the formal interview stage, it is still important to answer the concerns of all applicants. In a few cases, nervous applicants changed an interviewer's opinion because they asked such penetrating questions.

11 Do not make commitments you cannot keep.

Be careful not to promise an interview as a way of getting off the phone or avoiding a question. Remain in control of the interview. More than one employer has gotten in trouble by making a promise that was undeliverable.

12 Explain the rest of the selection process.

Before closing the conversation, be sure the applicant understands what is next. One of the greatest sources of irritation for applicants is not knowing when or how a decision will be made. Remember, applicants may also be customers.

Evaluating Callers

It is essential to record information immediately after each screening call. The hustle of most businesses makes us forget most of what we hear within a couple of hours. Here are some quick tips for making the most of the information you gather:

- ➤ **Complete the evaluation immediately.** Remain seated and fill out the form as best you can. Waiting to fill in the information for two or three applicants at the same time only makes the information run together.

- ➤ **Be consistent in your evaluations.** You may feel compelled to be more generous with applicants you liked, but this has to remain a business decision. Their ability to get along well with others should be noted, but not given undue weight. On the other hand, a person with excellent qualifications should not be penalized for seeming nervous on the phone if dealing with people is not a significant portion of the job.

- ➤ **Write complete thoughts.** A jotted note may be difficult to decipher two or three days later. The quality of your notes has a direct impact on your ability to make an accurate decision.

- ➤ **Confine your comments to business necessity.** Remain focused on how well the applicant matches the job requirements. The fact that he would make a great shortstop for the company softball team is irrelevant. Besides being inappropriate information to record, it also could be questioned should your notes be reviewed following a discrimination complaint.

- ➤ **Be careful what you write.** In addition to irrelevant material, take care to avoid comments that infer discrimination. The words "older woman" written on an evaluation simply to help you recall who's who of the many applicants could be questioned as bias against those covered by the Age Discrimination in Employment Act.

- ➤ **Follow through on commitments you make to the applicant.** Once the evaluation is complete, make sure to send any information you promised the applicant along with investigating questions he asked for which you had no immediate answer. Your prompt follow-up demonstrates your commitment to hiring the best.

Interviewing
Effectively

50

Establishing the Interviewing Process

Interviewing is the method recruiters rely upon most heavily for selecting new employees. It is also the most difficult to master. The typical interview consists of questions about the applicant's work history, education, desires, and skills. But there is more to an interview than just what questions to ask. The non-verbal communication between the screener and the candidate, the depth of the answers, and a host of other factors all create a picture to use in evaluating employees. To help prepare yourself for conducting an interview, fill out the Interview Priority Checklist on page 53.

To make the most of interviewing candidates, you must first establish a process that can be followed consistently.

Who Will Conduct the Interviews?

Those conducting the interviews should have a direct role with the position. Likely candidates include the position's direct supervisor, the supervisor's boss, and perhaps managers who have substantial contact with the person in the position.

> **How many rounds of interviews will there be?** Refrain from making a marathon out of the process. More than three interviews is probably counterproductive. Different interviewers should ask different questions. Asking the candidate to respond to the same questions over and over accomplishes little.

> **When will the interviews take place?** Select a schedule for hiring and stay with it. Everyone conducting the interviews should clear their calendars in advance of scheduling candidates. Following a consistent timetable with all applicants sends the message that the position is important.

> **Where will the interviews take place?** Consider different options. You can conduct the first interview in a manager's office. The second interview might take place in a factory setting if you're a manufacturer, or in a store if you're a retailer. Watching candidates react to the environment they may be working in can reveal a lot about them.

> **What information do you want to learn from each candidate?** Define in advance the information you need to make clear decisions. You are making an important decision based on these interviews. Ask what you need to know.

> **What purpose will each round serve?** Determine in advance why you need each round of interviews. In many cases, two rounds will suffice. Do not make the mistake of conducting the first round with 20 candidates. This elongates the process of narrowing the field. If you do have an extraordinary number of qualified people, conduct a round of phone screenings before asking anyone to the office.

> **How will screening decisions be made?** Decisions should be made in a clear and organized fashion. Develop a simple evaluation form that can be used by everyone involved. While gut feeling plays a role in any decision, attempting to quantify your criteria as much as possible makes for a clearer outcome and probably a more successful decision.

INTERVIEW PRIORITY CHECKLIST

Position: _____   Dept.: _____

Using the job description as a reference, list the skills and characteristics you feel the successful candidate needs to possess. Be sure that every factor you list is job related. When you have listed all skills and characteristics, weight each according to its level of importance to the success of the job. When you have completed this form, use it to develop interview questions and screening tools for the selection process.

1 = low   5 = critical

Priority	Skills and Characterics	Weight

Total Weight =

Questions to Ask

The questions you ask and how you ask them largely determine the outcome of any interview. Therefore, these questions should be carefully designed to solicit as much information as possible.

Remember that all questions should be job related. Even simple discussions about a candidate's spouse or children can be construed as seeking discriminatory information. If you think you're asking something discriminatory, you probably are.

As you begin to develop questions, review the job description to determine the actual criteria you will use to make a selection. These criteria should provide you with the basis for most questions.

Be sure to include a question about aspirations. While a candidate's ideas may not totally match what you had in mind, their answers will shed light on levels of ambition, focus, and enthusiasm. How the candidates see your job fitting into their plans has a great deal of influence on their desire for the position. Ask candidates to tell you why they are interested in the position. Their answers are a window into their understanding of the position, the match with their skills, and whether they researched your organization.

Questions about education should revolve around how a candidate's training applies to the position. Again, you must be careful about appearing discriminatory. It is not a good idea, for example, to ask cashier applicants about their writing skills, since the ability to express oneself on paper is not a significant part of the job. On the other hand, you may ask whether they believe that courses they have taken contribute to the skills needed for the job.

Questions about experience also must be job related. Base your questions on how they performed in a position, not just what they did. Give them situations to solve and pose questions that make them think about how the problem could be solved in your environment. Whether they answer the question the same way you would is irrelevant; it's how they arrived at their solutions that counts.

In addition to questions about goals, education, and experience, you may ask about work habits and attitudes. How well does the candidate get along with others? Will this person fit into your work environment? Is this person flexible and adaptable? You may be able to glean quite a bit regarding these characteristics from the way other questions are answered. Review the list of Sample Interview Questions in the back of the book to get you started.

For more ideas on interview questions, read *Behavior-Based Interviewing* by Terry Fitzwater, a Crisp Series book.

Consider the Setting

In addition to developing questions, you should consider the setting in which the interview will take place. A lot of distractions and noise inhibits your ability to concentrate. While a plant or site tour might be appropriate on a second interview, during the first meeting it is better to be in an environment where you can concentrate on what the candidates say.

Try to prevent interruptions during the interview. Interruptions destroy concentration, and candidates may interpret such distractions as a message that you don't care. If interruptions cannot be prevented in your office, find another location.

If you do plan on a plant or site tour, arrange it in advance. It is embarrassing to arrive on site only to discover that the guide was not informed or there is nothing going on that can be observed. Once again, disorganization sends the wrong message.

In any interview, begin by putting the candidate at ease. As in any unfamiliar situation, the candidate will be somewhat uncomfortable. A little small talk, the offer of a beverage, or a light joke helps ease the tension.

Conducting the Interview

Begin by outlining the process. Explain the sequence of events that will happen in the interview. Refrain from defining the amount of time you will spend. If things are not going well after 15 minutes into a 45-minute interview, it may be difficult to end if you have stipulated the time as 45 minutes.

> **Keep an open mind.** Your first impression of a candidate is usually lasting, but don't let it overshadow everything else in the interview. Some very good candidates may be nervous and give a less than positive impression until they relax.

> **Let the candidate do the talking.** Refrain from talking so much about the job or company that the candidate gets little opportunity to talk. The more people talk, the more insight you will gain into their personalities.

> **Be careful not to explain questions as you're asking them.** You may give away the answer without knowing it. Stick to short, open-ended questions such as, "How do you describe your leadership style?"

> **Remain attentive.** When you are conducting a series of interviews, it is easy to get distracted by other concerns or by fatigue. Do not let boredom overtake you. Take notes while the candidate is talking. What you write down will help you recall events later on.

> If you feel that you are losing attentiveness, try paraphrasing what the candidate says. The candidate might say, "My last boss left a lot of things up to me." In response to that, you might say, "So you had a lot of responsibility."

> By paraphrasing, the candidate knows you are paying attention and you are involved in the conversation without dominating it. In addition, this technique encourages the candidate to expound on whatever you paraphrased, giving you even more information.

> **Observe body language.** Besides listening to what is said, watch how it is said. Is there a level of enthusiasm? Does the person ask a lot of questions? Is there good eye contact? Does this individual sound invested in the job? Nonverbal actions represent the majority of communication, so attune yourself to these factors.

➤ **Maintain control.** Be careful not to allow the candidate to take over the interview. Some enthusiastic individuals may attempt to get the better of you by asking lots of questions or making editorial comments rather than answering the questions.

In other situations, you may let time get away from you. Stick to the schedule unless there are extraordinary circumstances.

➤ **Probe incomplete answers.** Sometimes the answer offered does not address the question. You may wonder if the candidate is hiding something. Ask more questions to ferret out the information. This process may feel uncomfortable, especially if you catch the candidate in a lie. This is better, however, than hiring the wrong person for the job.

➤ **End the interview on a positive note, but without announcing a decision.** Keep your reaction to yourself and simply assure the candidate that you will be in touch within a short time.

➤ **Write an interview summary immediately after completing the interview.** Record your general impressions along with any questions or concerns you may have about the candidate. Waiting even one hour will greatly reduce your recall of the events. Use the Interviewer's Self-Rating Form on page 58 to help you evaluate your performance.

➤ **Consider alternative interview strategies.** For example, in addition to the traditional interview, some companies ask top management candidates to complete projects that demonstrate the ability for self-expression and organization. Others ask individuals to make presentations. Still others provide typical situations an employee might face and ask the candidate to solve the problem.

Some organizations are also returning to testing clerical skills, since these skills are becoming more complex. Too many organizations have been burned by individuals who said they could do something, but they really couldn't. Don't ask. Test!

Targeted selection systems, such as behavior-based questions, are also popular. Instead of saying, "Tell me about yourself," ask candidates to explain how they resolved a particular type of situation. Even if you do not agree with how the situation was handled, you gain insight into the person's problem-solving skills.

For more on improving your listening skills, read *The Business of Listening* by Diana Bonet, a Crisp Series book.

INTERVIEWER'S SELF-RATING FORM

Interviewer: _____ Date: _____

Candidate interviewed: _____ Position: _____

> 5 = Handled smoothly
> 4 = Handled well but needs refining
> 3 = Has a grasp but needs improvement
> 2 = Needs significant work
> 1 = Found this difficult

Rapport with candidate:

_____ Opened the interview and made the candidate feel at ease

_____ Avoided direct criticism of candidate

_____ Listened sympathetically

_____ Put the candidate at ease in awkward situations

Control of the interview:

_____ Developed questions in advance of the interview

_____ Maintained the focus of the interview

_____ Made smooth transition from one topic to another

_____ Allocated time appropriately

_____ Returned to the original question when answer evasive

_____ Paced interview well

Persuaded candidate to elaborate on responses by using:

_____ Follow-up questions

_____ Silence

_____ Paraphrases of applicant's initial response

Note taking:

_____ Took notes discreetly during interview

_____ Did not allow note taking to interfere with interview

_____ Noted dress and appearance if relevant

_____ Reviewed and summarized notes for follow-up

Interviewing While Walking Around

Walking candidates around the workplace is a powerful alternative to the sit-down interview. Interviewing while walking around reveals all kinds of subtle indicators you cannot elicit from a formal interview. Here is a short guide to this approach:

➤ **As you approach the person to be interviewed, watch him for subtleties.** How does the person look before he realizes you are watching? What is this person's posture? Facial expression? Is there eye contact with others?

➤ **After greeting the candidate, suggest that the two of you go for a walk around the workplace and talk at the same time.** While he was probably expecting a sit-down interview, there is no choice but to comply.

➤ **Watch the person walk.** Does he keep up with you? Do the eyes wander? Is the person easily distracted by all the activity?

➤ **As you walk with the applicant, ask the questions you have prepared.** While the applicant may have had a pat set of answers prepared in return, walking around may throw him off his pace. That's what you want. You want the truth, not the rehearsed stories. Most people can't walk and lie at the same time, so listen closely to the content, not how well the story or answer is given. Truth is more important than polish. If you're uncertain of the person's answer, bring the subject up again later in the interview.

➤ **Introduce the candidate to several members of the staff. How is the eye contact?** How is the handshake? Does the person appear to treat women differently than men? Do you get a feeling of warmth and sincerity? Don't do this just once. Do it several times. Then take an average. See how each employee responds.

➤ **Walk the applicant into the area of the organization where he would be working.** Watch the reaction. Does he appear interested? Don't listen to the words; watch the eyes. Get the applicant involved with the area in which he might work. Watch the reaction in each situation. Does the person catch on quickly? Ask thoughtful questions? Does he pitch in? Watching a person in the actual workplace is useful in judging his future performance.

Selling the Organization's Image

Part of your job in an interview is to sell candidates on working for your organization. Communicate the organization's best point. You might even want a "cheat sheet" to refer to when describing the company. Make sure any recruiting literature you have is polished and professional.

Be prepared to respond to candidate questions. Put yourself in the place of your candidates for a second and understand how they might think. The candidates you want will ask the toughest questions because they care the most and have done the most research.

For more ideas, read *50 One-Minute Tips for Recruiting Employees* by David Hayes and Jack Ninemeier, a Crisp Series book.

Promoting the Company

As has been stated earlier, employee selection is not a one-sided event. Promoting your company is important in attracting high-caliber candidates. Read the example below.

Selling Points of Our Company

As much as the candidates are trying to convince us to hire them, we need to persuade the top candidates to work for us. The points below provide some information on the company that makes us more attractive to work for. While it is important to sell the company, make sure you sell it to the right people. Try not to lead applicants on and be careful about making commitments you or the company cannot keep.

In explaining the company, have you mentioned that:

➤ We are a growing company with plenty of upward potential. Our revenues increased more than 50% per year for each of the last three years.

➤ Our benefits program covers eye and dental care and there is no employee contribution, other than a $15 copay per visit.

➤ We have a stock ownership program for all employees.

➤ We reimburse employees for all classes completed at approved colleges, provided they achieve a grade of "B" or better.

➤ We are considered one of the largest suppliers of cleaning equipment and supplies on the East Coast.

➤ We offer flextime for a number of our positions.

How would you promote your company to potential applicants? List your company's selling points here:

1. _____

_____

2. _____

_____

3. _____

_____

4. _____

_____

5. _____

_____

Evaluating the Candidates

Once the interviews are over, it is time to make some decisions. The best way to do this is to develop a simple evaluation sheet as you did for reviewing applications and résumés. An Interview Evaluation Form is provided on the next page as an example. Outline the criteria across the top and the candidates' names down one side. In some instances, one or two candidates will stand out above the rest and the decision will be obvious. In other cases, it will be a close call. You cannot pass everyone on to the next round.

Be careful to avoid bias. Candidates should be evaluated on their merits as related to the job criteria. While there is room for some gut instinct, it should not overrule other important information.

Be timely in making decisions. Stay with the schedule you have announced to the candidates. Falling behind due to distractions or uncertainty can be costly when your best candidate takes another job or accepts a position with your competitor.

INTERVIEW EVALUATION FORM

Applicant: _____   Phone: _____

Applying for: _____

Interviewer:_____   Date: _____

List in priority order all the skills and characteristics necessary to perform the job.
This information should be taken from the interview priority form. When you have completed
this form, make a copy for each candidate to be interviewed.

1 = Unacceptable for this position   5 = Exceeds requirements

Required Skills/Characteristics	Rating

Total Rating =

Preferred Skills/Characteristics	Rating

Total Rating =

PART 5

Testing

66

A Requisite of Employment

While still controversial in some cases, many businesses include pre-employment testing in their battery of hiring tools. Pre-employment testing can be divided into two categories—psychological and physical.

Psychological Screening

Psychological screening determines an applicant's skills, honesty, and attitude toward work. So-called paper-and-pencil tests are generally applied near the beginning of the selection process and are used to eliminate applicants prior to the first round of interviews. These tests take many forms and some are relatively inexpensive to use.

Physical Screening

Physical screening determines fitness to perform on the job. These tests include screening for drugs and alcohol, AIDS, and genetic disorders. Where paper-and-pencil tests are conducted at the beginning of the process, physical screenings are generally conducted at the end as a condition of employment. In other words, "We would like to offer you the job, but you must pass the physical screening first." The purpose of this timing is to avoid invasion of privacy complaints and to reduce costs.

Testing should serve a specific purpose in your hiring process. It is a reliable method for selection in some instances, but it can be costly and time-consuming. Further, with much of its legality still to be decided by the courts, testing can be a legal landmine unless thoroughly researched and closely monitored. Since it can be assumed that little, if any, information can be kept truly confidential in any organization, the risk of a breech of confidentiality can also pose challenges.

Testing can run from $3 to $400 per incidence depending on the type and accuracy of the method. This may be prohibitive for some companies. Many organizations that require drug and alcohol screenings ask the applicant to submit to a physical prior to employment, since placing the screening within the examination diffuses some of the controversy.

Before including screening in your selection process, you must develop a clear understanding of its role and desired outcomes. The three major considerations in the use of testing are legality, cost, and organizational reasoning. Let's examine each.

Legality

Testing must pass the hurdles of validity, business necessity, and potential adverse impact. Validity means that the test must measure what it is supposed to measure. Packaged tests for skills, honesty, and personality have been validated before being placed on the market. An employer also must be able to demonstrate that the skills or characteristics measured are a business necessity. For instance, you may not require a retail store applicant to pass a writing test unless you can demonstrate that there will be extensive writing required on the job. Also, the tests must not have a disparate impact on protected groups.

Legalities of drug screening:

> ➤ There are no federal laws regulating drug screening.

> ➤ Currently, California, Connecticut, Iowa, Minnesota, and Vermont are the only states with state laws regulating drug screening, although several others are debating it. Consult with counsel before introducing such a program.

> ➤ Employers within the jurisdiction of federal, state, or local antidiscrimination laws may risk disparate impact. (In other words, the screening has an unfair impact on one or more protected classes of applicants.)

> ➤ Unionized employers should recognize that the initiation of a drug-screening program must be included in collective bargaining.

Cost

While a $3 drug screening or honesty test may seem inexpensive, these expenses can add up when coupled with other considerations. On the side of physical tests, inaccuracies as high as 50% are common with less expensive drug screenings. This requires a confirmation screening that is more accurate, but also more expensive. Over a one-year period, this can run into thousands of dollars.

Screening a large number of applicants with paper-and-pencil tests is a common practice among some companies, but these tests can also run up the costs. Add all of these costs together and testing becomes a significant part of your recruiting budget.

Organizational Reasoning

Finally, each organization must closely examine its motive for testing before beginning any program. What is the purpose of the screening program? What precipitated it? What are the expected outcomes? Is the organization committed to close monitoring and confidentiality? Are there legal ramifications that could cause time and expense? Is there an equally effective alternative?

Paper-and-Pencil Tests

Paper-and-pencil tests can be broken into three categories:

- ➤ Honesty and personality

- ➤ Skills and aptitude

- ➤ Dependability

Honesty and Personality Tests

Honesty and personality tests are used to determine an applicant's tendency toward honesty and how well the person would get along in the job and work environment. Skills and aptitude tests measure one's ability to perform certain tasks such as typing, math calculation, and writing.

Accuracy has been the main controversy surrounding these tests. Some critics maintain that applicants who answer too honestly may be disqualified, while individuals who know how to manipulate the tests will be accepted.

Applicants who do not test well are sometimes disqualified when they would, in fact, make excellent employees. Additionally, tests that fail a higher number of people from protected groups than is the average for all groups are considered discriminatory.

Finally, critics also maintain that pre-employment screening is an invasion of privacy and point to interviews, résumés, and applications as a reasonable means of gathering information.

Written honesty and personality tests began to be used more widely after employers were denied the right to use polygraph (lie detector) tests as a pre-employment screening device. While they are not foolproof, studies have found a strong correlation between those who are considered "high risk" by the tests and those who were found to steal on the job.

The tests usually consist of multiple-choice, true-false and yes-no questions. The tests come with a booklet and answer sheet and range in price from $5 to $14. There is usually a built-in "lie scale" to determine whether an applicant is trying to manipulate the test. A question of this nature might be, "I never think about stealing something from my employer." Since it is assumed that some temptation to steal passes through everyone's mind at one point or another, a person who answers true might be attempting to manipulate the test.

Handwriting analysis is a device for personality screening that is gaining acceptance in the United States. Popular in Europe for years, handwriting analysis reviews the physical characteristics of one's handwriting compared with correlated samples from other people. Critics argue that this technique has no scientific basis. Handwriting analysis runs from $25 to $400.

Skills and Aptitude Tests

Skills and aptitude tests measure the applicant's ability to perform a task or use a skill. Where honesty and personality tests generally consist of standardized instruments, skills and aptitude tests are a combination of published tests such as a typing battery and tests created by the employer to measure a specific skill.

You, as the employer, must be very careful to make sure that the tests you develop are valid and non-discriminatory. These tests do not have to be written in form. They might be physical measures such as coordination, lifting, and assembly.

In order to be valid, a test must pass one of the three validation techniques approved by the Equal Employment Opportunity Commission's guidelines for validation. Check with your local district office for additional information.

If you choose to conduct pre-employment honesty, personality, and skill testing, follow these recommendations:

> ➤ Check federal and local regulations on pre-employment testing before proceeding.

> ➤ Check references of testing services and the companies that supply the materials.

> ➤ Make sure that each test you use measures what you want it to measure.

> ➤ Be sure that all testing is validated, especially those created by your organization.

Dependability Tests

Dependability tests are used to forecast an applicant's likelihood of success on the job. These tests are adaptations of what industrial psychologists have termed "trait testing." As such, they evaluate an applicant's attitudes, practices, and values that are job-related, as compared with a so-called cognitive test that attempts to measure reasoning and learning.

A dependability test specially designed for a company is validated to show that there is a clear relationship between a particular test result and job performance. These tests evaluate a variety of values instead of honesty alone.

Each company must score its own tests, since the tests are developed specifically for that organization. Some companies have a pass-fail cut-off; others have a system allowing for a range of scores. Subjective judgments and other factors are usually incorporated into the hiring process as well. These tests work best for businesses that have many employees and experience a high turnover of non-management personnel.

The cost of developing these tests is generally $20,000 and up. But each company owns the test developed for it and the cost of each administration declines with use. For a firm with 3,000 employees, for example, the average cost of the test can be approximately 30 cents per applicant.

Drug and Alcohol Tests

Recent studies indicate that drug and alcohol screening has gained acceptance among American employers. This is largely due to an effort to increase productivity and decrease absenteeism and accidents on the job.

The controversy over drug testing revolves around invasion of privacy, inaccuracies, and workplace safety. Regardless of your feelings about drugs, as the employer you have a legal responsibility to maintain a safe workplace while remaining within the law.

At this point, there are no federal laws governing testing for drugs or alcohol. While some states have legislation regarding an applicant's rights to privacy, none has specifically prohibited drug testing. It is best to consult with your attorney before commencing with pre-employment screening for drugs and alcohol.

The procedures for testing are rather complex, but a basic understanding of the concepts is helpful.

Most employers screening for substance abuse use urine testing. More sophisticated methods involve blood, breath, skin, hair, or saliva.

Laboratories that provide these services commonly use "enzyme multiplied immunoassay," which measures the reaction of the urine specimen to radioactive animal antibodies. This reaction indicates a presence of drugs.

The most accurate of these tests is the "gas chromatography mass spectrometry" (GC-MS) test. This is used to confirm the presence of drugs, since many initial screenings have such a high error rate. Any applicant who tests positively should be given an opportunity for a confirming test to assure accuracy, even if it is at the applicant's expense.

Drug screenings can identify other medications the applicant is using for such conditions as depression or epilepsy. Be careful not to evaluate applicants based on this information, since it may be an invasion of privacy or protected under handicap legislation.

The selection of a laboratory is a crucial part of any drug-screening program. Be careful to check references and ask to see the facilities in which the work is done. It is important to execute an agreement emphasizing confidentiality. This contract should contain a "hold harmless" clause making the laboratory, and not your organization, liable for negligence in the event of litigation.

When deciding whether to conduct pre-employment drug and alcohol screenings, follow these guidelines:

➤ Conduct screenings as part of an overall physical.

➤ Check laboratory references thoroughly before proceeding.

➤ Test only those who have reached the final stages of selection.

➤ Have all applicants sign a release. Make sure they understand their refusal means automatic elimination from consideration.

➤ Applicants who fail the drug screening should be eliminated on the basis of not passing the physical.

➤ Absolute confidentiality must be maintained at all times.

Performance-based Testing

Performance-based testing is an alternative to drug screening. Though generally administered to current employees, it warrants mention in this chapter. This type of testing requires employees to pass a daily test demonstrating various abilities required for performance on the job. These might include visual acuity, hand-eye coordination, reflex timing, and other elements of physical fitness. The technology generally involves a computer-based video game requiring employees to pass a test before going on the job.

Companies using this type of testing include trucking and taxi firms and entertainment or tour companies requiring professional drivers. The applications are widespread and are a viable alternative to drug screening.

Performance testing measures immediate impairment from sources ranging from drugs and alcohol to fatigue, stress, and emotion. Testing for impairment provides employers with an evaluation of an employee's actual physical and mental state at the time of work, as opposed to drug testing, which requires a significant waiting time for results. Performance testing can be done every day without raising questions of privacy. Performance-based testing generally costs less than $1 per employee per episode. If performance testing catches on, it will provide an extremely viable alternative to the more controversial drug screening.

Deciding Whether to Test

Simply considering the idea of pre-employment testing may create controversy within your organization. While honesty or skills screening might be fully accepted, testing for drugs is sure to stir issues. The best way to deal with potential controversy is to determine in advance your reasons for testing, along with the goals you wish to reach by using it. Is it to reduce theft, increase productivity, reduce absenteeism, or create a safer work environment?

Whatever your reasons, develop a clearly defined and consistent plan. Nothing alienates applicants and employees more than inconsistency in policy. It also opens you up to possible litigation and fines.

For more information, read *Personnel Testing* by John W. Jones, a Crisp Series book.

Medical Screening

Requiring a physician's examination, regardless of whether you are screening for drugs, is sound advice. Some applicants suffer from preexisting conditions such as back and head injury. Have your company physician examine all new employees. The cost of exams should not be a consideration, since the long-term effects of not doing so can be devastating.

However, conditions found during the examination may not be used to refuse employment unless the job for which the applicant has applied would cause her harm, or the employer can demonstrate that the applicant cannot perform the functions required. It is permissible for an employer to ask any applicant to demonstrate how she would perform certain critical tasks of the job should the employer have a concern. An example of this is asking an applicant with a hearing impairment to demonstrate how she might hear orders on a factory floor. In the event that the applicant is capable of performing the critical elements of the job, it is in everyone's best interest to come to a reasonable accommodation on secondary elements the applicant may have trouble performing. In the hearing impairment example, a special device might be installed on the factory floor to allow this individual to communicate adequately with others.

The Americans with Disabilities Act forbids medical screening of applicants prior to an offer being made. However, all job offers should be made with the contingency that the candidate passes the physical.

PART 6

Conducting

Reference Checks

Overcoming Obstacles

How often do you check the references of applicants you are seriously considering? It takes time and effort. And then you usually hear only glowing recommendations and praise. It's easy to conclude that all this investigating is a waste of time; still, you can glean valuable candidate information.

In addition to getting biased information, another issue is the reluctance by some companies to provide information beyond employment dates and job titles. In this litigious society, an applicant who feels slandered can sue a former employer for negative comments.

Still, reference checking must play a crucial role in the selection process. It is not enough to rely on the applicant's word, but getting the right information can be a challenge.

Resistance from References

Obtaining reference information used to be fairly easy. You called the former supervisor, asked a few questions, and received candid answers.

Over the past decade, however, a number of employers have been sued successfully by former employees who claimed that the references had made false statements about their performances. As a result, many employers examined their practice of giving references, and a number of them developed policies prohibiting the release of information other than the employee's dates of employment and job title. Calls to supervisors for references often result in the caller being referred to the human resources department.

To overcome this resistance, several strategies may be attempted:

➤ If you call the employee's department and are referred to human resources, try the department again later. A different person may answer the phone who will be willing to give out information.

➤ If you are having little success, ask another member of your department to give it a try. Sometimes the rapport developed between the reference checker and reference giver makes all the difference.

➤ You might also call back and simply ask to speak with a person who has worked with the applicant. With an open question like this, you may get a willing response.

➤ Finally, if nothing else works, appeal to the reference's common sense. If all companies stop giving references for fear of being sued, the recruiting system will experience a grave loss.

Questions to Ask of Former Employers

Preparation is the key to making the most out of a reference check. This inquiry must be conducted in a deliberate fashion. Questions should be developed from examining the job description and reflecting back on individuals who have held the position. All questions should be job related. Drifting into inquiries about lifestyles and personal information is asking for trouble.

There must be consistency between candidates. Asking different people different questions destroys your ability to compare. While all queries should be consistent, you should pursue inconsistencies in what the reference says, and seek clarification if a response arouses your curiosity.

How to Ask Questions of References

Because of time pressures, there may be a temptation to rush through reference checks. Yet building rapport is one of the most important parts of conducting this type of inquiry. The impressions you get will be just as important as the facts. It is your job to make the references feel at ease. The more rapport you build, the more information you can obtain. Discipline yourself to hear not only what is said, but also how it is said.

Some references may be more hesitant to provide information than others. They may not, for instance, feel positively about the person in question. If you get an indication that they feel reluctant about certain topics, these may be areas you should pursue with other references and the applicant.

One means for getting additional information out of a reluctant reference is to rephrase the question:

> **Q:** *"How would you describe this employee's work ethic?"*
>
> **A:** *"She did her job . . . got along with people."*
>
> **Q:** *"So would you say that she approached her job with energy and enthusiasm?"*
>
> **A:** *"Uh . . . I guess you could say that."*

In the exchange above, the first query did not get the desired results. So the questioner drew a conclusion to see how the reference would respond. While the reference verbally agreed with the conclusion, it was obvious that it lacked sincerity.

In this case, the questioner could pursue the response by saying something like, "You don't sound too enthusiastic about this employee." But this tactic may offend the reference by challenging the original response. If the questioner wants to obtain additional information on other topics, it is best to maintain the rapport and drop the question.

In some cases, you can manipulate a reference's impressions to obtain the information you need. You can say, "We're down to our finalists, and are trying to get the best match." From this statement, references may conclude that they have nothing to lose and therefore will be more candid in their responses.

A similar question might be, "Since this person will be going through some training once she's on board, I'm wondering where you think she would benefit the most?" If the reference draws the conclusion that the applicant already has the job, that person might be more forthcoming with relevant impressions. It is up to you, as a reference checker, to provide many opportunities for the reference to open up. Remember, it is not just what is said, but how it is said.

Which of the following might you ask of references? Add others that will help with your candidate search.

- ❏ How long did the employee work for the company?
- ❏ What position did the employee hold at the end of the tenure?
- ❏ What position did the employee begin in?
- ❏ How would you describe the employee's work ethic?
- ❏ Given the opportunity, would you hire the employee again?
- ❏ What reservations should I have about hiring this person?
- ❏ This is what the person would do for our firm. How do you think this person's skills and abilities would fit into that position?
- ❏ Who else within your organization would be able to comment on this person's performance?
- ❏ What were the reasons given for leaving your organization?

   Others:

   _____

   _____

   _____

Evaluating References

Once you have spoken with the references of all finalists, it is time to compare the results. Again, the key here is to remain impartial and consistent. If copious notes are taken during each reference check, you should have an accurate picture of how each candidate interacts with an employer, the reservations the employers have, and the points in favor of each candidate. Remember to include the non-verbal clues of the references in the evaluation. These sometimes form the key information on which to come to a conclusion.

Reference checking is performed in the final stages of selection, so the information you receive should serve to confirm conclusions already drawn on finalists. If, however, you receive information about a candidate that needs checking, pursue it. Requesting additional contact with a finalist may be uncomfortable, especially if this person appears to be the best choice, but you need to address all questions before making a decision.

Credential and Credit Checks

In addition to checking references, you may wish to verify other credentials. These might include education, training and credit.

It is not uncommon for some applicants to exaggerate their educational credentials. Do not fool yourself into thinking that because a candidate has all the right answers that they also have the credentials. While most do, all should be checked. Some schools will release transcript data only at the written request of the student. If this is the case, impress upon the applicant that you need the material promptly to expedite the hiring process.

When calling educational institutions, go a couple of steps beyond asking whether the applicants actually attended. Ask if they graduated and when. Check to see that the majors a candidate indicated on the application can be verified.

Credit checks are appropriate only when the position being filled involves money or major fiscal responsibility. In other words, you may check the credit of a controller or cashier, but not a production manager or sales person.

The **Federal Fair Credit Reporting Act** regulates this information, as do many state laws. Consult with your attorney regarding what may be done in your locale.

Credit information tells you whether the candidate is experiencing financial difficulties. From these facts you may determine whether this person might be tempted to handle funds illegally or indiscreetly. This practice protects your against in-house loss and theft, as well as actions brought by others while the employee is acting in your behalf.

P A R T 8

Decision Making
and Offers

Matching the Candidate to the Criteria

How clear is your decision-making process for hiring? Whether you are selecting a chief executive officer or a cashier, decisions should be made carefully. Holding the fate of someone's job in your hands is not an easy task. You must make sure that both the organization and the employee are well served.

As you approach the final decision on which candidate to hire, it helps to revisit the original criteria for the best candidate. There is a chance that you have not found a perfect match. You may decide to reopen the search for candidates who better match the position's needs. If you have done a good job recruiting, however, the next group will not be any closer.

The better strategy is to compare the job description to your best two or three candidates. Flexibility is the key to making a successful hiring decision successful. Searching endlessly for the perfect match is usually unrealistic and does not serve your organization well.

Here are some guidelines for making a final decision.

➤ **Develop another comparison form similar to the ones you created earlier in the selection process.** See the Candidate Selection Form on the next page for an example.

➤ **Maintain consistency when making decisions.** Once all the information has been gathered, only those making the decision should be involved. Discourage outside lobbying.

➤ **Recognize that strict job criteria is not the only consideration.** Every decision-maker must trust a little "gut feeling." The new employee must be able to thrive in the environment and get along with others on the team. These factors are sometimes not clearly defined or demonstrated in job descriptions and interviews.

➤ **Be able to explain your decision.** Chances are you will be asked to justify your pick by a supervisor or co-workers. Your ability to clearly delineate your reasons will quell any uncertainty about the decision.

➤ **For clerical and labor positions, one decision-maker is optimal.** This person should be the position's immediate supervisor. For managerial jobs, a maximum of three persons should be involved. This should include the immediate supervisor and two other individuals with whom the person will work.

CANDIDATE SELECTION FORM

Position: _____ Start date: _____

Supervisor: _____

Applicant's name: _____ Phone: _____

Qualifications required	Comments	Rating

Qualifications desired	Comments	Rating

Evaluator: _____ Date: _____

For more information on finding the best candidate for your job opening, read *Quality Interviewing* by Robert Maddux, a Crisp Series book.

Securing the Best

With increased demand for skilled employees, it is important to develop effective strategies for landing your best candidates. Here are a few hints to enhance your hiring success:

- ➤ **Share as much information as you can with your top applicants.** Give them an opportunity to get to know your organization in depth.

- ➤ **Establish a common interest.** Ask candidates about their desires, goals, and aspirations. Discover their values and what they consider important. The more you are able to match their needs with yours, the better the match will appear to them.

- ➤ **Organize your negotiating stand ahead of time.** Consider all aspects of the package, including vacation, salary, benefits, perks, budget control, influence on their destiny in the company and so on. Be prepared at all times to discuss the compensation and role that person will play in the organization.

- ➤ **Use your intuition.** If something feels wrong about a candidate, investigate. Better to uncover unpleasant facts now rather than later.

- ➤ **Use your sales pitch!** Be prepared to persuade your top candidate. Don't go overboard and overwhelm. But try to convince this person that this is a good match.

- ➤ **Don't make promises you can't deliver.** No candidate is worth exceeding the bounds of common sense. If you're being asked for something you truly can't deliver, say so. Look for alternatives to satisfy the candidate's desires.

- ➤ **Act quickly!** The best candidates wait for no one. Keep the selection process moving, and keep your top candidates informed. The more they are involved in the process, the more they will be invested.

Notifying Candidates

Notifying candidates is one of the most crucial parts of the selection process. Remember, candidates are examining you just as you are examining them! Timely execution of the decision reassures your top applicants of your interest and renews their interest in the position.

Keep the process efficient by announcing a schedule to all candidates. This discourages the procrastination sometimes associated with selection. The entire process for any candidate should take no longer than three weeks.

Motivate in-house personnel by selling them on how productivity will increase and their time commitments will decrease once the new person is on board. Keep them abreast of the process. If there is a delay in the process, call the finalists to let them know they're still being considered.

All applicants should be notified in a consistent manner. Everyone should be treated the same to avoid the appearance of bias or unfair treatment. Further, treating finalists consistently and openly leaves a good impression. You never know when your paths may cross again.

Every applicant who has been interviewed should receive a response. If eliminated, candidates should be notified within a week. Notification should take the form of a letter. Using post cards, as some employers do, is embarrassing and insensitive. A sample rejection letter is included below as an example.

Dear _____

Thank you for your interest in the position of _____ our organization.

We received a great number of applications from qualified individuals and we have made a decision.

We will keep your application on file for six months in the event other applicable openings arise. Thank you for your understanding. We wish you the best in your job search.

Sincerely,

_____

Making the Offer

Timing is an important part of making an offer. Once a decision has been made, contact that person immediately. More than one hiring opportunity has been missed by delaying for a day or two.

Once you make the offer, confirm it in a letter. You will find an example of an offer letter on the next page. Be careful not to include language that implies permanence or a guarantee of lifetime employment. All employees should be referred to as "current" or "full-time," not "permanent." In the letter, state the starting date, compensation, where to report, and other specifics. Welcome the candidate into the organization.

With highly skilled candidates and upper management you will probably negotiate at least a portion of the agreement. Here are a few tips:

➤ **Know your parameters before discussing the offer with the candidate.** Develop a list of possible offering points and stick to your plan. Don't "wing" the negotiations. It will cost you money and maybe the candidate.

➤ **Use incentives as bargaining points.** There are a host of options from which to choose. In addition, you may tie compensation to performance, enabling the candidate to earn significantly more.

➤ **Consider non-monetary perks.** These might include a larger office, more control over vacation and other days off, latitude in project selection, and influence in decision making.

➤ **Get the candidate to commit before making the offer.** Your job posting may have asked for salary history or requirements, in which case you have a rough idea of the candidate's expectations. You may ask the candidate, "What do you think you're worth?" The response to this question will provide insight into how well the person has researched his or her own worth and how realistic the expectations are.

Dear _____

We enjoyed the opportunity to meet with you this past Wednesday. We are pleased to offer you the position of _____.

This offer is contingent upon the following:

- A satisfactory physical exam

- Proof of authorization to work in the United States (Please bring these documents with you on the first day of work.)

Accepting this offer means that you will be performing the following duties and be responsible for _____. Your salary would be $_____ monthly.

I hope you will accept this offer. We feel our organization provides excellent opportunities and working conditions along with a comprehensive benefits package.

I would like to have your decision by _____. If you have any questions, feel free to call me at _____. I look forward to your reply.

Sincerely,

_____

Refusals

Regardless of how hard you try, your top candidate may refuse the offer. If you have not received a response within two days of the offer, phone the candidate again to answer any questions and confirm an understanding of the offer.

If the candidate holds out for more compensation, you will have to negotiate. Be prepared before making this follow-up call. If more than one candidate is declining, you might want to reconsider your package and compensation. Ask candidates why they declined, and you may receive some useful information.

S U M M A R Y

Closing Thoughts

High performance hiring is the only alternative for companies to excel in the future. Trial-and-error staff selection is no longer effective. Integrate employee selection functions into your everyday duties.

Always be on the lookout for talent and enthusiasm. Have clear knowledge of all positions under your authority. Be prepared to hire individuals quickly and decisively. Selection does not have to be an elongated process. Attack employee selection with energy and focus.

Attracting attention to your company also attracts applicants. Continually polish corporate image. Be prepared to talk about the organization and possible openings. If someone shows interest, conduct an informal interview. If you like what you see, ask for some contact information. You may be unaware of an opening right now. . .but it might be waiting for you when you return to the office. So keep your candidate files up-to-date. Work to create the corporate image necessary to attract applicants. Be *the* company to work for, and you will have your choice of the top performers.

High performance hiring requires investment. But like all good investments, it pays off in the long run with a rich selection of applicants.

Hiring is just the first step in establishing an effective workforce. For ideas on keeping employees happy and productive, read *Retaining Your Employees* by Barb Wingfield and Janice Berry, a Crisp Series book.

High Performance Hiring Checklist

Use this checklist to develop a game plan for high performance hiring. Some of these pieces may already be in place where you work, but success requires completion of the formula!

❏ Can you clearly explain your organization's hiring philosophy? (i.e., "Since our industry is prone to high turnover, we concentrate 40% of our recruiting budget on promotions and community activities to keep our name in front of possible applicants. We reward long-term workers to keep them motivated.")

❏ Do you have up-to-date job descriptions for all positions you supervise?

❏ Are you able to explain current openings to prospective candidates?

❏ Do you have an understanding of federal legal requirements and the intent of the law?

❏ Are you knowledgeable about local and state legal requirements?

❏ Have you identified applicant motivations for the positions you hire for?

❏ Have you developed a system for reviewing résumés that uncovers the information you need?

❏ Have you developed a system for reviewing applications that uncovers the information you need?

❏ Do you have a system for deciding on finalists after the applications and résumés have been reviewed?

❏ Have you developed a system for checking references?

❏ Have you developed a system for checking credentials and credit if applicable?

❏ Have you defined the information you need from an interview and established a process that uncovers this information on a consistent basis?

❏ Are the others involved in the selection process clearly trained on interview techniques and application review?

❏ Have you developed a system for selling organizational image when in contact with clients?

❏ Have you established a process for making interview decisions?

❑ Have you examined the option of whether to test applicants and make a determination?

❑ If you use tests, have you developed a reliable system for achieving the data you need?

❑ Have you developed a system for making final decisions, making offers, and negotiating compensation?

❑ Do you periodically review your hiring process for improvements and stay up-to-date on new techniques and legal requirements?

Sample Interview Questions

A list of questions that may be asked during an interview follows. Remember that all inquiries must be job related.

Work Experience

➤ What do you consider your greatest accomplishment in a work environment and why?

➤ Why do you think you were successful?

➤ What is the single most important idea you have contributed to your present job?

➤ How do you go about making important decisions?

➤ Describe the relationship between you and your present boss.

➤ What are your boss's title and functions?

➤ What are the duties in your present job?

➤ What percentage of time do you spend on each duty?

➤ What type of supervision do you have?

➤ What is the biggest frustration in your present job?

➤ Describe the reporting structure in your present job.

➤ With whom do you deal on a regular basis within your office?

➤ Do you supervise others? How many?

➤ Describe your supervision style.

➤ What do you most like doing in your present job?

➤ If you had the opportunity to change two things at your present job, what would they be?

➤ What was the most difficult task you have had to complete?

➤ If I asked your bosses to evaluate your performance, what would they say?

➤ Why do you wish to leave your present job?

Education and Training

➤ Have you graduated from high school?

➤ What was your grade point average?

➤ Are your grades a fair reflection of your work? If not, why not?

➤ Have you attended college?

➤ What did you study?

➤ Have you completed your course of study?

➤ What courses did you do best in? Why?

➤ What courses did you have the most trouble with?

➤ What courses did you dislike the most? Why?

➤ Were you involved in extracurricular activities? If yes, which ones?

➤ What did you like best about school?

➤ Do you feel your education was worthwhile?

➤ Would you pick the same course of study again?

➤ How did you happen to change to a different school?

Military Service

➤ Why did you enlist in the military?

➤ Why did you choose the branch you did?

➤ What was your rank or grade?

➤ Did you ever consider a military career?

➤ Why did you decide against it?

➤ What type of assignments did you perform in the military?

➤ Why did you leave the military at the time you did?

The Job in Question

➤ Why did you apply for this position?

➤ What do you know about our company?

➤ What appeals most to you about this job?

➤ What strengths do you bring to this position?

➤ How does this job compare with other positions to which you are applying?

➤ How does this job fit into your career plans?

➤ What did you do on your last job to make yourself more effective?

➤ If you were hiring someone for this position, what qualities would you look for?

➤ How does this position compare to positions you have filled in the past?

➤ If you are hired, what kind of attendance record can we expect?

➤ Is there anything that will hinder you from getting to work on time?

➤ What reservations should I have about hiring you?

Personal Traits

➤ Tell me three characteristics about yourself?

➤ What makes you different than other candidates?

➤ What motivates you?

➤ What are your career goals?

➤ Why do you think you would be successful in this job?

➤ What was the best job you ever had? Why?

➤ Who was the best boss you ever had? Why?

➤ Do you like working as part of a team?

➤ What do you consider important in a job?

➤ Are you most comfortable leading or following? Why?

➤ Is there anything you'd like to add about yourself that we have not discussed?

➤ Do you have any questions about the job or our company?

Additional Reading

Andler, Edward C. *The Complete Reference Checking Handbook*. NY: AMACOM, 1998.

Bonet, Diana. *The Business of Listening, Third Edition*. Crisp Series, 2001.

Dickson, Mary B. *The Americans with Disabilities Act*. Crisp Series, 1995.

Fitzwater, Terry L. *Behavior-Based Interviewing*. Crisp Series, 2000.

Hayes, David and Jack Ninemeier. *50 One-Minute Tips for Recruiting Employees*. Crisp Series, 2001.

Jones, John W. *Personnel Testing*. Crisp Series, 1994.

Ling, Barbara. *Poor Richard's Internet Recruiting*. Lakewood, CO: Top Floor Publishing, 2001.

Maddux, Robert B. *Quality Interviewing, Third Edition*. Crisp Series, 1994.

Simons, George. *Working Together, Third Edition*. Crisp Series, 2002.

Steingold, Fred S. *The Employer's Legal Handbook, Fourth Edition*. Berkeley, CA: Nolo Press, 2000.

Visconti, Ron and Richard Stiller. *Rightful Termination*. Crisp Series, 1994.

Wendover, Robert. *Recruiting for High Performance*. Crisp Series, 2003.

Wendover, Robert. *Smart Hiring: The Complete Guide to Recruiting Employees*. Naperville, IL: Sourcebooks, Inc., 2002.

Wingfield, Barbara and Janice Berry. *Retaining Your Employees*. Crisp Series, 2001.

Other Resources

Periodicals

HR Magazine
Society for Human Resource Management
606 N. Washington St.
Alexandria, VA 22314
(703) 548-3440

Workforce Magazine
245 Fischer Ave., Suite B2
Costa Mesa, CA 92626
(714) 751-1883

Inc. Magazine
38 Commercial Wharf
Boston, MA 02110
(617) 248-8000

Employment Practice Reference Sources

Bureau of National Affairs
9435 Key West Ave.
Rockville, MD 20850
1-800-372-1033

Business and Legal Reports
141 Mill Rock Road E.
Old Saybrook, CT 06475
(203) 245-7448

CCH Inc.
4025 W. Perterson Ave.
Chicago, IL 60646-6085
1-800-835-5224

Dartnell Inc.
360 Hiatt Drive
Palm Beach Gardens, FL 33418
1-800-621-5463
(561) 662-6520

Equal Employment Opportunity Commission
1801 L Street N.W.
Washington, DC 20507
(202) 663-4900

Personnel Forms

Amsterdam Printing & Litho
Wallins Corner Road
Amsterdam, NY 12010
(518) 842-6000

Dartnell Inc.
360 Hiett Road
Palm Beach Gardens, FL 33418
1-800-621-5463
(516) 662-6520

Selectform Inc.
P. O. Box 3045
Freeport, NY 11520
(516) 623-0400

Written Honesty Tests

ETS Test Collection
Educational Testing Service
Rosedale Road
Princeton, NJ 08541
(609) 921-9000

Reid/London House
9701 W. Higgins Rd.
Rosemont, IL 60018
1-800-221-8378
(708) 292-1900

Pinkerton Services Group
13950 Ballanty N E
Corporate Place, Suite 300
Charlotte, NC 28277
1-800-528-5745

The Reid System
153 W. Ohio
Chicago, IL 60610
1-800-922-7343

Stoelting Co.
620 Wheat Lane
Wood Dale, IL 60191
(630)-860-9700

Written Personality Tests

Bay State Psychological Associates
225 Friend St.
Boston, MA 02114
1-800-438-2772
(617) 367-8400

Consulting Psychologist Press
3803 E. Bayshore Road
Palo Alto, CA 94303
1-800-624-1765
(415) 969-8901

Reid/London House
9701 W. Higgins Rd.
Rosemont, IL 60018
1-800-221-8378
(708) 292-1900

Personnel Decisions, Inc.
45 S. Seventh Street
Minneapolis, MN 55402-1608
1-800-633-4410
(612) 239-0927

Stoelting Co.
620 Wheat Lane
Wood Dale, IL 60191
(630) 860-9700

Employment History Verification

Fidelifacts
42 Broadway, Rm. 1548
New York, NY 10004
(212) 425-1520

Verified Credentials, Inc.
20890 Kenbridge Ct.
Lake Ville, MN 55004
1-800-473-4934

Also Available

Books•Videos•Computer-Based Training Products

If you enjoyed this book, we have great news for you. There are over 200 books available in the *Crisp Fifty-Minute™ Series*. For more information visit us online at www.axzopress.com

Subject Areas Include:

Management
Human Resources
Communication Skills
Personal Development
Sales/Marketing
Finance
Coaching and Mentoring
Customer Service/Quality
Small Business and Entrepreneurship
Training
Life Planning
Writing